INTRODUCTION TO
ARISTOTLE'S THEORY OF BEING AS BEING

INTRODUCTION TO ARISTOTLE'S THEORY OF BEING AS BEING

by

WERNER MARX

translated by

ROBERT S. SCHINE

MARTINUS NIJHOFF / THE HAGUE / 1977

Translated from the original German edition: *Einführung in Aristoteles' Theorie vom Seienden*, Freiburg im Breisgau, 1972.

ISBN 90 247 1941 0

PRINTED IN BELGIUM

TABLE OF CONTENTS

TRANSLATOR'S NOTE

The translator is much indebted to Dr. Joyce Hoy, for her many improvements to the style, to Mr. Thomas Nenon, for his assistance in reading the proofs, and to the author, for his assistance throughout the translation of this book.

FOREWORD

Philosophy finds itself "between tradition and another beginning." [1]
For this reason it seems necessary to reconsider the foundations of
traditional philosophy in the hope that out of these considerations new
questions may arise which may lead to a new philosophical foundation.
To this end neither the large manual nor the monograph is well suited.
What is required, instead, is to take a few steps which lead our thoughts
directly into the problems of a given, traditional, philosophical foundation.

In this sense the present work wishes to provide an "introduction"
into that philosophical foundation which, until Hegel, had a decisive
influence upon traditional philosophy. Consequently, it does not see
its task in providing a survey of this whole complex of problems. Nor
does it offer solutions to questions about difficult passages which have
been the subject of two thousand years of Aristotelian scholarship.
Instead, it follows a definite path which might bring this Aristotelian
science, the theory which seeks to determine being *as* being, *on hei on*,
closer to the student of philosophy.

Freiburg im Breisgau   WERNER MARX
April 1977

---

[1] Cf. by the author: *Reason and World: Between Tradition and Another Beginning*,
The Hague, 1972.

PREFACE

This introduction is limited to a single theme of Aristotelian philosophy, namely, the science (*episteme*) of being as being, the science which is regarded as the foundation of traditional philosophy and which, in addition, has always been one of the main concerns of Aristotelian scholarship. Aristotle defined the object of this science in Books Alpha, Epsilon, Kappa, Lambda, and also in other passages of his metaphysics.[1] Only in book Gamma, however, did he discuss more thoroughly the program of this one, particular science, the program which necessitates that it be only one science. There, in Book Gamma, he defined more precisely the nature of its object. This is one of the reasons for which we will take this book of the metaphysics as our point of departure. By doing so we gain a first insight into the "program" of the theory of being as being; at the same time, a series of questions arises which can serve as an outline for this treatise.

Gamma 1 begins:

There is a science (*episteme*) which contemplates (*theorei*) being as being (*to on hei on*) and that which belongs to it per se.[2]

This programmatic statement leads to the following questions: What does Aristotle mean by "knowledge" without qualification? What does

---

[1] The work traditionally called the *Metaphysics* was not conceived of by Aristotle as one work. Instead, it consisted of a series of independent, shorter writings which were first brought together into one work by later editors. The title "Metaphysics" was derived from the book's position in Aristotle's works as a whole, namely μετὰ τὰ φυσικά (after the Physics). Initially, therefore, the meaning of the title had no bearing on the contents of the book itself.

[2] *Meta. Γ* 1, 1003 a 21 f. Ross translates: "There is a science which investigates being as being and the attributes which belong to this in virtue of its own nature." Note: In this text the translations by W. D. Ross (*The Works of Aristotle translated into English*. Oxford, 1908, 1928²) are given in the footnotes only when they differ greatly from our own.

he mean by "science" (*episteme*)? Finally, what is characteristic of that knowledge and that science which contemplates "being as being"?

The very next sentence answers these questions only insofar as it distinguishes the science in question from other sciences in one particular respect.

This is not the same as any of the so-called particular sciences; for none of these others treats universally (*katholou*) of being as being. They cut off a part of being and contemplate what belongs to this part (*to symbebekos*) as for instance the mathematical sciences do.[3]

The specific difference is thus "universality." The other sciences address themselves to a particular generic unity, and they proceed in such a way as to subsume the objects of their inquiry under particular classes. None of them treats of being "universally," as does the science in question here. But how are we to understand the universality in the procedure of this unique science?

Does Aristotle mean that this science investigates a multitude of species? Or does he have in mind a particular manner of approach or a particular characteristic of the object under investigation? What, for example, is the difference between the theoretician of physics, the *physikos*, and the theoretician who inquires into being as being? To be sure, later passages in Book Gamma give some indications of how to answer these questions,[4] but a more thorough answer can be given only within the framework of an inquiry which begins with a definition of what Aristotle means by knowledge and proceeds from there to a characterization of that which is peculiar to philosophical knowledge and its objects. Therefore, following the course cited above, the first part of the present treatise will attempt a definition of this particular science.

The introductory sentence from Gamma 1 quoted above already referred to the subject matter of the theory in question here: being as being. But what is the meaning of the word "being" (as a participle)? Does this term refer to "being" in general, to that which is universally "being," or only to that which is "being" in a particular way? And what does Aristotle mean by the word "as" (*hei*) in the formula "being as being" (*to on hei on*)? The very next sentence appears to answer this question:

Since we are seeking the principles and highest causes, it is clear that these are necessarily and essentially of a certain nature.[5]

[3] *Ibid.*, a 22-26.
[4] Cf., e.g., *Meta. Γ* 3, 1005 a 33 ff.
[5] *Meta. Γ*1, 1003 a 26-28. Ross translates: "Now since we are seeking the first

PREFACE

But what do the terms "principles" and "highest causes" mean? And above all, what is this "nature" whose principles and causes are supposed to be sought? The next section does not respond to these questions either, but is does give an important clue to the Aristotelian way of philosophizing.

If then those who searched for the elements of beings (*ton onton*) were seeking the same causes, then the elements must have been elements of being, not by accident, but of being as being. Therefore, it is of being as being that we also have to grasp the first causes.[6]

Earlier thinking had searched for the necessary basic elements of being. These basic elements are among the causes of being. From this Aristotle concludes that the early thinkers were already seeking the elements of being "as" being. He acknowledges again his obligation to follow his great predecessors and likewise to seek the first causes of "being as being." Instead of expressly defining the subject matter of the science of being as being, Aristotle shows by this recourse to tradition how such an inquiry is possible and necessary. The whole of book Alpha of the *Metaphysics* had already attempted to show that the inquiry into first principles and causes is not a new beginning, but only the logical continuation of the thinking of Aristotle's predecessors. Likewise, here in book Gamma, the subject matter of the science in question is justified by demonstrating that the question of being as being is a continuation of the ancient question of first principles.

Such a justification, however, does not represent a definition of the science, and it is just such a definition which seems to be at issue in the introductory chapters of book Gamma. Is this definition to be found perhaps in the sentence quoted above, which states that these principles and highest causes are "of a certain nature"? Indeed, the task of the first section of the second chapter of book Gamma is to define this "nature" explicitly; how this is accomplished will be shown later.

In any case, a further reason for our beginning with book Gamma is this: in none of the other books of the *Metaphysics* which deal with being as being did Aristotle attempt such a definition. We believe we can show that the justification for introducing this theory as an "ontol-

principles and the highest causes, clearly there must be something to which these belong in virtue of its own nature."

[6] *Ibid.*, a 28-32. Ross translates: "If then those who sought the elements of existing things were seeking these same principles, it is necessary that the elements must be elements of being not by accident but just because it *is* being. Therefore it is of being as being that we also must grasp the first causes."

ogy," whose meaning then discloses itself as that of an "ousiology,"
lies in that "nature" whose principles and highest causes are being
sought. The question of whether and to what extent this ousiology has
a theological character will be raised at the conclusion of our inquiry.
But first of all, what is the "certain nature" whose principles and
highest causes are being sought?

The second chapter begins:

Being (*to on*) can be said in many ways, but all-that-is is related to a unity
(*pros hen*) and one certain nature (*physis*) and is not *homonym*, but is related
in the same way that everything which is said to be healthy is related to health
either in that it preserves health or in that it is a symptom of health or in that
it is capable of it. And that which is medical is related to the medical art
(either it is called medical because it knows the medical art or because it is the
work of the medical art) and just as we find other things said in many ways,
similar to these examples, so can being be said in many ways, but all related
to one principle. Some things are called being because they are *ousiai* (substances), others because they are affections of *ousia*, others because they are a
process towards *ousia*, or productive or generative of *ousia* or of things which
are spoken of as related to *ousia* or negations of one of these or of *ousia* itself;
it is for this reason that one even says of non-being that it is non-being.[7]

As he often does, Aristotle proceeds here from the assumption that we
can speak of something in a variety of ways. Thus being also appears
in our speech in manifold ways. Under close scrutiny it appears that
because of a definite "dependent relationship" (see p. 18), all these
diverse ways are related to a certain, single "nature." Aristotle calls
this one, eminent unifying concept (*Inbegriff*) "*ousia*," essence, substance
(see p. 20).

Everything which can be called being is being in that it either is *ousia*
itself or is related to *ousia* in some manner, for instance, as its quantity
and quality, its generation or destruction, its negation, and so on.
Ousia appears as the point of reference underlying the various meanings
of "being." It is "the one, certain nature." But what does *ousia* mean?
Aristotle tried to answer this question in the form of a science which
is not only assertive, but which seeks principles as well. The inquiry
beginning with Gamma 1 concerns the *episteme* which inquires into
being as being and therefore, ultimately into *ousia*.

A science presupposes, however, that it has an area of investigation

---

[7] *Meta. Γ* 2, 1003 a 33 - 1003 b 10. This translation follows that by Ross, with
some significant differences. Throughout the *Metaphysics*, Ross renders *ousia* with
substance.

which can be clearly circumscribed. Can *ousia* be grasped in this sense
as the point of reference for the manifold meanings of "being"? Is it
able to unify the area of investigation of this science? We read:

Just as there is *one* science which deals with everything related to health, so
it is with the other sciences. Not only is it one science which contemplates the
kath'hen legomena (that which, in its relationship to a common genus, represents
a structured unity) but it is also one science which contemplates that which
is related to *one* nature (*pros mian physin*), for even this, in a way, is related
kath'hen. Thus it is clear that the contemplation of being as being belongs to
one science. Every science is concerned chiefly with that which is primary,
that on which everything else depends and to which it is related. If this primary
something is *ousia*, then the philosopher should address himself to principles and causes of *ousia*.[8]

At this point the train of thought is concluded. The science concerned
with being as being addresses itself to these principles and causes. As
now becomes apparent, however, it deals with an area of inquiry which
receives its unity from a primary principle, from a certain nature, *ousia*.

Two groups of questions emerge from what has been discussed so
far. The group discussed above concerns the area of investigation of
the science in question. Part Two of this inquiry will deal with these
questions by considering how Aristotle develops the theory of being as
being with regard to *ousia* in books Zeta, Eta, and Theta. Following
this, Part Three will consider the problem of the "relationship" of this
"ousiology" to "theology," whose object, especially in book Lambda,
is that unique *ousia* which Aristotle understands to be God and the
divine.

This book concludes with an attempt to determine the significance
of this theology for ousiology. First, however, in Part One that series
of questions must be clarified concerning the concept of *theoria*: What
is knowledge? And above all, what kind of knowledge develops into
science, and finally into that science which in its perfected form — that
is in the form of the highest *theoria* — is able to contemplate "being
as being"?

---

[8] *Ibid.*, b 11-19.

KNOWLEDGE, SCIENCE
AND PHILOSOPHICAL THEORY

Knowledge of being as being was defined in Gamma 1 as *episteme*, science, but more precisely as knowledge which addresses itself to its object contemplatively, "theoretically." Theoretical knowledge is connected with the other two fundamental types of human activity which Aristotle also calls knowledge, with poetical knowledge, that is, knowing how to produce something, and with practical knowledge, which can be called knowing how to act. Whereas *poiesis* and *praxis* are each concerned with a particular end beyond knowledge as such, theoretical knowledge has its end in itself; it is knowledge for the sake of knowledge.[1]

Unclouded by any exterior purpose, this type of knowledge satisfies the demand inherent in itself in a higher sense, the higher in rank, the more general, and finally, the more "being" the object is towards which it is directed. The highest theory is that knowledge whose object is being as being and the principle and causes belonging to it. It is that knowledge — as shall be set forth later — which addresses itself to the highest being, God (*theos*). The theory second in rank is the science of nature which investigates movable or changeable beings, that is, the realm of "composite" being (*synholon*). Finally, mathematical science considers being with regard to its quantitative characteristics.[2] The two latter sciences exhibit a related structure. They investigate a certain part of being (as in physical theory, i.e., physics) or a certain aspect of being (as in mathematical theory). In each case, the respective science begins with principles and concepts [3] which are primary and indemonstrable,

---

[1] τοῦ εἰδέναι χάριν, *Meta.* A 2, 982 a 15; cf. also *Nic. Eth.* K 7, 1177 b 1 ff. b. 20; *Meta.* A 1, 981 b 17 ff.; A 2, 982 b 25.

[2] On this tripartite division, cf. *Meta.* E 1, 1026 a 7; K 4; K 7, 1064 b 1 ff.

[3] Cf. *An. Post.* A 2, 71 b 19 ff.

that is, principles and concepts which are irreducible and necessarily true and evident. From there it proceeds to derive, to explain, and to demonstrate the diverse things belonging to the respective science's subject matter. Thus, these sciences are apodictic.[4]

What, then, is the difference between these two apodictic types of philosophical theory and that highest-ranking, first theory which investigates being not in a limited domain or in a limited aspect, but being in so far as it is being? Here two differences should be emphasized which are especially important for the question at issue:

1. First of all, the whole of the knowledge constituting these theories represents a framework of principles or laws which are classified according to their greater or lesser degree of universality. This framework is a likeness, so to speak, of the inner structure of the corresponding realm of being in its "whatness," a structure which is essentially generic (see p. 15). On the other hand, the all-inclusive nexus of being as being does not exhibit such a generic structure (see p. 17 ff.). It encompasses not a particular realm of being but every being insofar as it is being. Its area of inquiry, moreover, represents what is usually called Aristotelian "metaphysics." [5] Thus, this knowledge is also not the kind of science which proves its propositions, as Aristotle has shown for physical and mathematical science in the *Posterior Analytics*. Since the universality of any propositions about being as being is not a generic universality, the purpose of this knowledge cannot be to derive, by means of systematic deduction, less general from the most general propositions. Instead, these propositions can be immediately attributed to every being, for the very reason that it is being. Here, therefore, knowledge will only have the task of bringing these characteristics to the fore and presenting them in their interaction. Their more exact meaning will become clearer in Parts Two and Three.

2. The second difference between the highest theory and the other two theoretical sciences concerns its relationship to its principles, that is, its specific type of thinking. Even those sciences whose knowledge

[4] *Eth. Nic.* Z 3, 1139 b 29-32.
[5] As an equivalent of the term "metaphysics" the title "First Philosophy" is often used. This usage is documented in Aristotle's writings: *Phys.* A 9, 192 a 35; B 2, 194 b 14; compare also *Meta. Γ* 2, 1004 a 2-9; *De An.* A 1, 403 b 16. In numerous passages in the *Metaphysics* where Aristotle speaks of *prote philosophia* (in E 1 and in the parallel passage in K 4) he identifies it with *episteme theologike*. With regard to the question whether this *prote philosophia* can be equated with the science of *on hei on*, and with regard to this problem in general as well, see Part Three of this book.

is limited in rank and scope cannot exhaust their work in deductive proof. They must also possess knowledge of the indemonstrable "origins" (*archai*, or principles) which make these sciences possible at all. But what kind of knowledge is this? "From the principle of the scientifically knowable can neither scientific knowledge, nor technical ability nor ethical insight arise." [6] If, by scientific knowledge,[7] one understands apodictic knowledge alone, then for knowledge of the original principles (*archai*), another kind of knowledge must be admitted, namely, the immediate apprehension of those first, necessary, and eternal principles by virtue of which all-that-is is, and thus those with which all knowledge aspiring to truth has to begin. The faculty of this immediate apprehension is intuitive understanding, *nous*. "The only remaining possibility," says Aristotle in the *Nicomachean Ethics*, "is that it is *nous* which addresses itself to the *archai*." [8] Only because *nous* complements scientific knowledge is the wise man able to "know not only what can be demonstrated, but also to state the truth concerning that which makes the demonstration possible." [9]

What for the other two sciences only augmented scientific knowledge in its narrower sense represents the distinguishing characteristic of knowledge for this primary and highest science. Because of this, this science, which addresses itself to the principles as such, is distinct from the other two. To be sure, philosophy in the strict sense of the highest theory also proceeds dianoetically, that is, by analysis, discourse, and judgement. Unlike in the genuinely apodictic sciences, however, *dianoia* is not the fundamental feature of the kind of thinking in question here. Rather, it plays only a subservient role. What characterizes the *theoria* concerned with being as being is that supreme human faculty which Aristotle also describes as the "divine in us" (see p. 10), the faculty of principles, *nous*. For Aristotle the term *nous* has a two-fold meaning.

---

[6] τῆς ἀρχῆς τοῦ ἐπιστητοῦ οὔτ᾽ ἂν ἐπιστήμη εἴη οὔτε τέχνη οὔτε φρόνησις *Eth. Nic.* Z 6, 1140 b 33 ff. Ross translates: "...the first principle from which what is scientifically known follows cannot be an object of scientific knowledge, of art, or of practical wisdom."

[7] In this context scientific knowledge, *episteme*, is one of the five ways of searching for truth. It refers more to a faculty of thinking than to a particular human activity, as is usually the case. Scientific knowledge in the latter sense of a particular activity includes the former as one of its aspects.

[8] λείπεται νοῦν εἶναι τῶν ἀρχῶν, *Eth. Nic.* Z 6, 1141 a 7 f. Ross translates: "...the remaining alternative is that it is *intuitive reason* that grasps the first principles."

[9] *Ibid.*, 7, 1141 a 17 ff. Aristotle continues: "Therefore wisdom must be intuitive reason combined with scientific knowledge — scientific knowledge of the highest objects which has received as it were its proper completion." (Ross translation.)

On the one hand *nous* denotes thinking, or the faculty of thinking in general; its activity can be described as "thinking, cognition, comprehension, opining, supposition, as well as discursive and intuitive thinking" (*phronein, gignoskein, manthanein, doxazein, hypolambanein, dianoeisthai, noein*). On the other hand, however, in the narrower sense *nous* is that specific part of the soul which characterizes the highest *theoria*, the knowledge of the wise man; it takes place in *noein, theorein*. Nevertheless, in the following we shall begin with *nous* in its broadest sense in order to be able to contrast this larger framework with an understanding of genuine philosophical *theoria*. We will inquire into the relationship between *nous* and perception, the specific object of *nous*, and the relationship of *nous* to truth and falsity.

According to Aristotle, *nous*, as faculty of thinking in general, that "with which the soul knows and supposes," [10] is closely related to the other parts of the soul. Above all, he presupposes that only in sense-perception are things immediately given to us. The way to the intelligible form (*noeton eidos*), to the object of thought, leads through the materially given sensible thing, the perceptible (*aistheton*), in which the thinkable is contained. What are the connections, or, specifically, the intermediate stages which lead from sensible perception to thought? Between perception and thought the intermediate stage is imagination (*phantasia*). It coordinates and "internalizes" what is perceived into an image (*phantasma*) no longer dependent upon the actual presence of an external object.[11] To this extent the activity of the imagination is subject to our will.[12] Nonetheless, as a sensible image, a product of the imagination retains the qualitative mark of the sensible. When thought makes use of these images, however, it is just this sensible quality to which it does not address itself. Its objects are the pure forms (*eide*), the essences (*ti en einai*) of the things (see below, p. 6). Thus thought, in its own right, must be capable of comprehension. Nevertheless, Aristotle compares thought, as a potentiality, with perception; at first both exhibit analogous structures. He characterizes thought in relation to its object as "passive, suffering" potentiality. By this he means a receptivity [13] which in thought, unlike in perception, which is dependent on the senses, cannot be

---

[10] Cf. *De An. Γ* 4, 429 a 23 λέγω δὲ νοῦν ᾧ διανοεῖται καὶ ὑπολαμβάνει ἡ ψυχή.
[11] Cf. *ibid., Γ* 3, 428 a 8.
[12] *Ibid.*, 427 b 17 f.
[13] δεκτικὸν...τοῦ εἴδους, *ibid., Γ* 4, 429 a 15.

impaired by the intensity of its object.[14] In this sense it is impassive, incapable of "suffering" (*apathes*).[15]

By applying the distinction between actuality and potentiality, one can distinguish between three types of thinking, also analogous to perception:

1. pure abstract ability (prior to learning, *prin mathein*, as in a newborn child),
2. knowledge, that is, the potential to actualize the known,[16]
3. actual thinking itself (*noein energeiai*).[17]

This kind of explanation, which draws a parallel between thinking and perception, differentiates between the two solely from the viewpoint of their respective objects. Clearly, however, the problem is how thinking grasps the given objects themselves, from the viewpoint of their capacity to be thought, and not from the viewpoint of their materiality or their particular qualities.[18] If this thinkable element were present in the given object as the perceptible element is, then there would be no need for two types of conception, one superimposed upon the other. The decisive difference between perception and thinking is this: perception has its object outside itself and its object sets it in motion (from without), whereas thinking, since its object is something thinkable, something intelligible, to this extent is always already with itself. As a potentiality, thinking is latently identical with what it thinks (*noeton*), always subject to the presupposition that the object of thinking cannot lie "outside" of thinking for the very reason that its object is not something given through the senses. Here the analogy with perception breaks down. If the object, the intelligible form (the *noeton eidos*), from the standpoint of its potentiality is nothing but "being-thought," then the actualization of thinking

---

[14] "After a strong stimulation of the faculty of sense we are less able to exercise it than before, as e.g., in the case of a loud sound we cannot hear immediately after, or in the case of a bright color or a powerful odor we cannot see or smell, but in the case of mind, thought about an object that is highly intelligible renders it more not less able afterwards to think objects that are less intelligible," *ibid.*, 429 b 1-6 (translation by T. A. Smith, in *Basic Works of Aristotle*, R. McKeon, ed., New York, 1941).

[15] *Ibid.*, 429 a 15.

[16] 429 b 5 ff.

[17] Cf. Theiler, *Kommentar zu De Anima*, Darmstadt 1966, p. 152.

[18] Thus, in a piece of meat the senses discriminate between the hot and the cold, a combination of material factors, whereas thought considers the pure form, the being of the meat (τὸ σαρκὶ εἶναι); cf. *De An. Γ* 4, 429 b 10 ff.

takes place in thinking itself. Taken in this way, it is only consistent that in the famous and notoriously difficult fifth chapter of *De Anima* Gamma, Aristotle posits so-called "active reason" (*nous poietikos*) next to the "passive reason" (*nous pathetikos*) (see below, p. 42). According to the beginning of this chapter, *nous poietikos* is related to *nous pathetikos* as form is related to matter (see below, p. 28 ff.). Understood as an ability, thought is purely passive in relation to what it is as actuality. Thus, for Aristotle, *nous* is mental insight occurring in utter immediacy into what admits of such "insight." Like perception, thought is also receptive. However, because of the peculiarity of its object as something not sensible, that is, as something intelligible, thinking reaches a completion different from that of perception: thinking and what is thought (*noesis* and *noema*) prove to be one and the same. Even though the being of thinking, as a human faculty, and the being of what is thought are not actually the same, nonetheless the distinguishing mark of this process of thinking consists in the very fact that "insight" (*noesis*) takes place in its unity and identification with what has admitted of such insight (*nooumenon*).

This *nooumenon*, the specific object of *nous*, is the non-sensible element in what is given by the senses. Thus, that which is capable of being thought in its primary and special sense is the intelligible form (*noeton eidos*) or that which forms a being. The *eidos* "man" is that which constitutes the common essence of all men. To this extent it is something "universal" (see below, p. 29). As an unanalyzed and indivisible thought, prior to all inquiry by means of predication or definition, the *eidos* grants certainty to thinking (see below, p. 24). Because such *eide* originally form a unity and not the product of a synthesis, Aristotle calls them "non-composite-essences" (*me synthetai ousiai*).[19] Thus the non-composite, universal, immaterial *eide* are to be regarded as the eminent intelligible objects of thought (*nooumena*). The *eide* in a narrower sense — as concepts of the essence of a being — represent only some of the concepts (*horoi*) which must be grasped before any judgement can be made. Generally speaking, these *horoi* are all those concepts of which one simply takes cognizance, such as the concepts "incommensurable" or "diagonal" before they are related to one another in a judgement. In the *Categories*,[20] Aristotle defined

[19] *Meta.* Θ 10, 1051 b 27. We refer here to the interpretation by K. Oehler: *Die Lehre vom noetischen und dianoetischen Denken bei Platon und Aristoteles.* Munich, 1962, p. 183 f. and 217 ff.

[20] *Cat.* 4, 1 b 25 f.

more precisely the various "kinds" of non-composite (*asyntheta*) and inseparable (*adihaireta*) concepts which can be part of a judgement.

Finally, the grounds or principles, the *archai*, of sciences also belong to the *noeta*.[21] Some of these principles are the fundamental concepts which determine the domain of each respective science. As such, they cannot be further reduced and become evident only when apprehended noetically. Others of these principles are the axioms basic to all thinking as such — above all, the law of contradiction [22] — or basic to particular special sciences, recognized in all thinking as the presupposed "being." And finally, the *archai* of being as such represent in a special way the aim of thinking for the highest philosophical theory.[23]

The faculty of *nous* could also be called a faculty of *truth*. This truth is peculiar in that it does not stand in opposition to falsity. In the case of noetic truth, there is no opposing pole, nothing which is untrue, no error, as the traditional concept of truth always takes for granted. This truth has nothing to do with adequacy - *adaequatio*. Instead there is only this alternative: either the noetic faculty becomes active and an object becomes present in it or it does not.

Thus, in Book Theta of the *Metaphysics* Aristotle writes: "Falsity does not exist, nor deception, but only ignorance — and not an ignorance which is like blindness; for blindness is akin to a total absence of the noetic faculty." [24]

What does truth mean, however, if it does not stand in opposition to "falsity"? How must thinking proceed in order that it be called a "true" intuitive apprehension? If "true" does not simply mean "not false," then the term must mean that in intuitive apprehension a thought emerges in its fulness and entirety and that the *noeton* thus becomes self-evident. But what is it that becomes self-evident? Nothing but what was inherent in the thought: the being itself revealed as it genuinely is. But what

---

[21] Aristotle deals with the *archai* and the role they play in the deductive sciences particularly in the first book of the *Posterior Analytics*.

[22] In *Meta. Γ* 3-6 the law of contradiction is expressed and discussed by Aristotle himself in the form which has been retained by tradition.

[23] Over against the threefold object of *noesis* presented above, the question could be raised whether a very significant *nooumenon* of *noesis* has been overlooked, namely, *noesis* itself. At that moment when thought reflects upon itself, does *noesis* amount to another distinct object of thought? *Noesis noeseos* is the formula Aristotle uses to designate the way the divine — and only the divine — *nous* works (see below, p. 45). How should this formula be understood? How did Aristotle himself understand it? The answer to this question can be given only in Part Three, where we shall define that line of thinking peculiar to God.

[24] *Meta. Θ* 10, 1052 a 1-4. The translation follows that by Ross, with some changes.

8 PART ONE

is genuine in the being? The simplicity (*haploun*) of its essence. The thought of essence — of the simple, the incomposite substance (*me synthetai ousiai*) — becomes absolutely and immediately present as a whole in the act of noetic thinking.

The "mental" content of essence presents itself in *noesis*, in contemplation, reason, intuitive apprehension in such a way that one can say that the essential content (*Wesensgehalt*) is real only in *noesis*. Aristotle defined this way in which mind meets mind — the apprehending and the apprehensible — as a "touching," [25] and not as a conception in the sense of active comprehension or grasping of something. It is the *noeton*, as the simple, undivided essential content which is originally present in *noesis*, the intuitive apprehension which perceives it, just as the intuitive apprehension is originally present in the *noeton* (see above, p. 5 f.). Thus, since the *noeton* is something which is "true," it is present in the *noesis*; for Aristotle, *noema* and *noesis* become the "same": in the act of apprehending a thing intuitively (*noesis*) that which is intuitively apprehensible (*noema*) becomes an intuitive apprehension (*nooumenon*). The *noeton* is nothing but the actualization of thinking, of *noesis*, and thinking is nothing but the thought (*noeton*),[26] which becomes a "true" apprehension because it is indivisible.

Nonetheless, in the realm of thinking there is also truth and error.

There, however, truth and error do not concern the apprehension of undivided concepts, of objects of thought as being immediately simple. They concern concepts insofar as they are composite and interwoven with one another: "In those cases where something can be true or false we always find a composition of the objects of thought which form a unity." [27] In thinking, one simple thought is set in relation to another, one predicated of the other, one connected with another by judgement. Such dianoetic thought, in the narrow sense, proceeds discursively; it combines and separates. Its object is no longer the "one," simple, indivisible, essential content, which is given or

[25] θιγεῖν, *ibid.*, 1051 b 24.
[26] On this subject see *De An. Γ* 4, 430 a 2 ff.; cf. also *Γ* 5, 430 a 19 f.; 6, 431 a 1 f.; 7, 431 b 16 f.; A 3, 407 a 7 f. *Nous* in action is identical with its objects, insofar as they are free of material — ἄνευ ὕλης: *De An. Γ* 4, 430 a 3; Cf. *Meta. Λ* 9, 1075 a 2 and on this passage: Hicks, *Aristotle's De Anima*, Cambridge² 1907; on 429 b 12, p. 486 and on 430 a 3, p. 497.
[27] *De An. Γ* 6, 430 a 27: ἐν οἷς δὲ καὶ τὸ ψεῦδος καὶ τὸ ἀληθές, σύνθεσίς τις ἤδη νοημάτων ὥσπερ ἓν ὄντων. J. A. Smith translates (*Basic Works of Aristotle*, ed. R. McKeon, N.Y., 1941): "Where the alternative of true or false applies, there we always find a putting together of objects in a quasi-unity."

"touched" in its immediate presence. Instead, it is the unity of a complex state of affairs (*Sachverhalt*) which becomes apparent only through meditation and "reflection." Dianoetic thought proceeds by combining or separating, by *synthesis* or *dihairesis*, because the complex state of affairs which underlies it represents a combination or separation itself.

This combining or separating of concepts in the judgements of dianoetic thinking is either true or false. Truth and falsity are possible not in things or states of affairs but exclusively in judgements. Only here can there be truth or error.[28] Nevertheless, this combining and separating is related to things and states of affairs. "Only he speaks the truth," Aristotle writes, "who thinks the separated to be separated and the combined to be combined, while he is in error, whose attitude is contrary to that of the things." [29] Thus, in order to be true, a judgement must "correspond" to the real state of affairs in all its complexity; it must "conform" to it.

This conception of dianoetic truth has had a long history. Truth of judgements as logical combination and separation (*synthesis — dihairesis*) was regarded as the truth as such. The meaning of truth as correspondence or adequacy became so decisive for western tradition, that throughout the centuries *veritas* has been conceived of as *convenientia* or *adaequatio intellectus et rei*. Whether one's point of departure was realistic or idealistic, this *correspondentia* was thought of either as the correspondence of the *res* to the *intellectus* or of the *intellectus* to the *res*. For Aristotle himself, the real combination or real separation of a thing or state of affairs was "pregiven." For him it was a matter of course that knowledge had to adapt to this reality, and moreover, that it was able to do so. Only through correspondence to this reality is dianoetic truth possible. In this sense, in *Met.* Theta 10 Aristotle says: "It is not because we correctly believe that you are pale, that you *are* pale, but because you are pale we who say this speak the truth." [30]

Having surveyed quite generally Aristotle's understanding of thinking

---

[28] Cf. *De Int.* 1, 16 a 12.

[29] *Meta.* Θ 10, 1051 b 3: ὥστε ἀληθεύει μὲν ὁ τὸ διῃρημένον οἰόμενος διῃρῆσθαι, καὶ τὸ συγκείμενον συγκεῖσθαι, ἔψευσται δὲ ὁ ἐναντίως ἔχων ἢ τὰ πράγματα. Ross translates: "...so that he who thinks the separated to be separated and the combined to be combined has the truth, while he whose thought is in a state contrary to that of the objects is in error."

[30] *Meta.* Θ 10, 1051 b 6. The translation follows Ross' version, with some changes.

and its thoughts, as well as the relationship of truth and thinking, let us return now to that kind of thought which is the actual concern of the present work, that is, to *sophia* (wisdom), to philosophical theory.

It was shown above that the highest of all human faculties, the faculty of thinking, is made up of dianoetic thought, that thought which articulates what is pregiven to it by separating and combining; and of noetic thought, which, preceding the specific articulation of the dianoetic, touches that in its object which is *nous*-like or the *nous*-like objects themselves. It was already pointed out above (p. 3 f.) that in a particular way this second and highest mode of thinking, noetic apprehension of noetically evident truth, must be regarded as the distinctive mark of the philosophical theory which contemplates being as being. *Sophia*, or philosophical wisdom, is the highest of all modes of cognition. However, its rank is determined by the fact that when it occurs, as the contemplation of that which is in itself *nous*-like, it becomes identical to the latter itself, as far as is humanly possible. For the more perfect its object is, the more perfect is contemplative thought itself. According to its inherent hierarchical tendency, that thought would be the most perfect which was least clouded by any admixture of the senses. It would be the pure contemplation of a purely noetic object.

Aristotle closely relates philosophical *noesis* with that activity which, for him, is peculiar to God alone (see below, p. 44). God is *nous*-like precisely because he is pure actuality, pure *energeia*, not clouded by anything sensible. When the *energeia* of pure thought and thus of immediate contemplation is taken as perpetual, it is itself something "divine." Thus it becomes clear how Aristotle could call *nous* itself, the highest form of human life, *theoria*, the "God in us." [31]

A philosopher is a person who emulates pure, divine thought and thus, so to speak, immortalizes himself.[32] Precisely this divine aspect of man represents for Aristotle the fulfilment of being-human in its highest and most perfect measure.[33] In this lies man's highest blessedness (*eudaimonia*). The thinking of a philosopher, however, can become similar to, but never equal to God. As something human it remains distinct from the divine, for it can never become pure *energeia*; it retains the character of potentiality (see above, p. 5), striving for fulfilment. Because of his transiency, the philosopher is deprived of the blessedness of per-

---

[31] ὁ νοῦς γὰρ ἡμῶν ὁ θεός, *Protreptikos* B, 110 (Düring).
[32] *Eth. Nic.* K 7, 1177 b 33.
[33] *Ibid.*, 1178 a 7.

petual contemplation. Philosophical thinking also remains transient because, as something human, it can never fully free itself from its fundamental reliance upon *aisthesis*, upon perception of the objects of sense as materially given. Philosophical thinking is bound to the *aistheton* but able to ascend from the *aistheton* to the *noeton*. This is the potential of a philosopher's thinking which distinguishes it forever from that of God. As something human, philosophical thinking is twofold: noetically turned toward the Simple-One, yet at the same time referring to the Sensible-Composite in its manifold conditions and relationships. Like every-day thinking it also is simultaneously noetic and dianoetic. It is directed toward noetic truth in a special way: through rational intuition it seeks the self-evidence of an essential content and seeks to dwell upon it. Nevertheless, for a determination of its object, as well as for an elucidation or exposition of it, philosophical thinking must rely on that thinking which combines and separates, dianoetic thinking. The documents of Aristotle's inquiries available to us show most clearly that the philosopher can in no way simply linger in pure contemplation; rather, the thought of the philosopher is characterized by question and aporia, by dialectic deliberation and refutation, by probing many possible solutions to a problem. It is thus an endeavor which always threatens to founder and which is always aware of this possibility.

However, there is still a decisive difference between philosophical *theoria* and the thinking of the common man. The *eudaimonia* of pure contemplation for its own sake [34] raises a man's goodness and nobility to its highest perfection. Theoretical thinking, taken purely as a process, is the highest thought because it is not clouded by any practical needs or purposes, just as its objects are more perfect and more real than the objects of everyday work and activity.

But more precisely, what are the objects of philosophical *theoria*? As we have seen, they must be the highest, most eminent being, for it is precisely the perfection of the objects of philosophical theory which accounts for the perfection of the theory itself. We need only to refer back to what we have already said about the human faculty of thinking in general. There we characterized the objects of noetic thought very generally so that now we need only ask which of them, as the highest objects, are the primary objects of the highest, the supreme thought, philosophical *theorein*.

Generally speaking, the objects of noetic apprehension were the

[34] Cf. *Eth. Nic.* K 8.

non-composite, simple empirical concepts which the mind must have already perceived in order to be able to relate them to one another by combination and separation. Neither more nor less than all human thinking in general, philosophical thinking must also accept these simple concepts, concepts representing the material, so to speak, of all the activity of the mind.

In a specific way these concepts are the *noeta eide*, as we already saw (see above, p. 6). We defined them as the non-sensible Simple-One, the essence, the forms of the sensible. Even with regard to these concepts, philosophical theory is not distinct from common thought.

Causes and principles were mentioned as a third object of thought. Of them, the first and most general constitute the actual and most eminent object of Aristotelian theory. Indeed, in *Meta.* Alpha 2 Aristotle showed that the peculiar object of *sophia* is that which surpasses all other being in universality and its capacity to be a cause or ground, (its primacy).[35]

Above all, this most universal something is that which we can call the "ontological principles"; for Aristotle, the "four causes," potentiality and actuality, substance, quantity and quality, being and unity are fundamental concepts of this sort. The science of being as being *per se*, of the totality of all-that-is, philosophical theory as primary and supreme knowledge in general, is a process of apprehension of the most general principles of all being.

The later so-called laws of thought are also of such a universal, fundamental character. These could also be called laws of being for Aristotle : in addition to the law of identity, the law of the excluded middle, and particularly the "law of contradiction": "It is impossible to assume the same thing to be and not to be at the same time."[36]

Finally, universality and the capacity to be a cause can be attributed in a third sense to those beings which are separated (*choriston*)[37] from all sensible admixture and thus, in being, surpass everything finite, those beings that are pure actuality, undimmed, simple being. These are the eternal "minds" (*noes*) (see below, p. 46 f.), the

---

[35] *Meta.* A 2, 982 a 8 - b 10.

[36] *Meta.* Γ 3, 1005 b 29. Ross translates: "It is impossible for the same man at the same time to believe the same thing to be and not to be."

[37] Aside from this usage of *choriston*, "separated," according to which the term means being separated from all sensible matter, the other usage of *choriston* should also be noted, according to which something is *choriston* which, as an individual and as something limited, exists independently; cf. on this topic particularly *Meta.* Z 3, 1029 a 28.

movers of the diverse celestial spheres, and above all, the prime mover, God (see below, p. 44). In these "eternal things" (*aïdia*) Aristotle sees the third eminent object of philosophical theory. In a certain sense, in this object of philosophical theory all being becomes simultaneously thematic, in that *theos* — as will be shown in more detail later — as the unmoved mover, is the *cause and keystone* of the entire universe.

PART TWO

THE OUSIOLOGY

In the *Corpus Aristotelicum* we repeatedly find the phrase *"to on legetai pollachos"*: " 'being' is said in many ways." For Aristotle the diverse meanings of fundamental philosophical concepts is not merely a burdensome consequence of imprecise use of language to be avoided whenever possible. Instead, it bespeaks the diversity of the things themselves. Moreover, an essential part of Aristotle's philosophy consists in attending to and explicating this diversity, and for him the manifold meanings of *"on"* undoubtedly are the most important. Recent scholarship has been particularly attentive to this essential problem.[1] In the preface we cited the beginning of the second chapter of Book Gamma and briefly discussed how he takes the manifold *"on"* as his point of departure and elucidates by two examples the particular way in which its manifold meanings are related to "one, certain *physis*":

...in the same way that everything which is said to be healthy is related to health either in that it preserves health or in that it produces health or in that

---

[1] Aristotle composed his own work on the *pollachos legomena* in which their diverse meanings are presented as a sort of lexicon of concepts. We read this work — which was continually revised by Aristotle — as the fifth (Δ) book of the *Metaphysics* (cf. Düring: *"Aristoteles, Darstellung und Interpretation seines Denkens."* Heidelberg, 1966, p. 593.) Its system of presentation betrays the old academic distinction between *onoma* and *logos* (cf. Topics, I. 15), which was then superseded by the Aristotelian principle of classification of the *pros-hen* relationship (in the case of "non-coincidental" homonyms). On Aristotle's relationship to language in this regard, cf. Kurt v. Fritz: *Philosophie und sprachlicher Ausdruck bei Demokrit, Plato und Aristoteles.* Darmstadt, 1966, p. 70 ff.; Specht, "Über die primäre Bedeutung der Wörter bei Aristoteles," *Kant-Studien* 51, p. 102 ff.; H. J. Krämer: "Zur geschichtlichen Stellung der aristotelischen Metaphysik. II. Zur aristotelischen Ontologie." *Kant-Studien* 58, 1967, p. 337 ff., see below n. 3. On the subsequent problematic, cf. further Fr. Brentano: *Von der mannigfachen Bedeutung des Seienden nach Aristoteles.* Freiburg, 1862, p. 83 ff., 108 ff.; J. Owens: *The Doctrine of Being in the Aristotelian Metaphysics*, Toronto, 1951, p. 55 ff., p. 151 ff.; F. Wagner: "Zum Problem des aristotelischen Metaphysikbegriffs," in: *Philosophische Rundschau*, 1959, p. 129 ff.

it is a symptom of health or in that it is capable of it. And that which is medical is related to the medical art (either it is called medical because it knows the medical art or because it is the work of the medical art)... [2]

Medicinal herbs, a doctor's art, the color of flesh, the human body — each of these objects appears to be something fundamentally distinct from the others. Each of them can be filed under and grouped in a different class of objects: the medicinal herbs under plants; medicine under the sciences; skin color under colors in general; and the human body under living bodies. Each one can be unequivocally defined by subsuming it under a more general rubric and by indicating the specific way in which it is distinct from the other things capable of subsumption under the same more general rubric. Thus, in this context Aristotle presupposes an interdependent nexus of generic classes into which every particular being can be classified (see below, p. 25). With regard to this genos-general term he speaks of the synonymous structure of a kath'hen: insofar as the diverse subordinate individuals or species are each related to a one (kath'hen), they can be spoken of as being the same. In this sense medicine, theology, and mathematics are kath'hen legomena, for something in common which is the same can be predicated of each of them, namely, that each of them is a science. Taken formally, it is of no consequence whether it be an individual or a species which is subordinated to the more general rubric. In each case it then remains to make specific differentiations of that which is more general, whether this be the species in relation to the individual, or the genus in relation to the species. Taken formally, the relationships man/Socrates and living thing/man are the same.

More specifically, for Aristotle it is this kath'hen structure that renders possible the generality, necessity, and absence of ambiguity which are the essential distinguishing characteristics of scientific knowledge. To this extent the generic unity of a particular nexus of Being appears to be the indispensable prerequisite for this nexus to be conceived of as the area of inquiry for a particular science. When Aristotle treats the manifold meanings of "healthy" or "medical" in the passage cited, he nevertheless has in mind the unified field of objects of a particular science — that is, without compromising the fact that the general class which is present here is not an all-embracing genos. The objects cited above — medicinal herbs, skin color and so on — are indeed generically distinct from one another, that is, they each belong to another *genos*; yet they can all be called "healthy." Health is not a common genus for all those things which can be said to be healthy; it does not provide the specific differences we need to arrive at the "species" medicinal herbs, medicine, and so forth. Instead, each of these objects can be called healthy in a fundamentally different way, that is, in a way not determined by its belonging to a structure of greater or lesser generality. Each of them stands in a different, *immediate* relation to "health" or "healthy." Accordingly, Aristotle speaks here of a *pros hen*-manifold which can be conceived of as a unity for the very reason that each of its objects is related to the self-same One.[3]

---

[3] Expanding upon the historically oriented initiatives of contemporary scholarship, H. J. Krämer (*loc. cit.*, see above, n. 1) has investigated the historical background of the structural relationship of the "*pros hen legomena*" more precisely, a relationship of great importance for Aristotelian philosophy. He comes to the conclusion that this structural relationship, which one is inclined to regard as being peculiar to Aristotle in contrast to the Platonic doctrine of the Ideas, actually lies — problem-historically speaking — in the continuity of the development of the metaphysics of the academy. Indeed, according to recent scholarship, Aristotelian philosophy has shown itself to be determined "much more strongly than supposed" by its provenance from common academic doctrine (p. 353 and n. 134, 135; for the connection between metaphysics and theology with Aristotle cf. below Part Three). One may assume with Krämer that an immanent, coordinated principle of structure and order manifests itself in the *pros-hen*-relationship, a principle standing in opposition to yet another principle which generalizes and subordinates, just as in the Platonic doctrine of the Ideas. The priority of an individual in which the whole is represented takes the place of the *genos* in the generic structure: thus, among the *onta*, the prominent ("primary") category of *ousia* would take over the function, so to speak, of a genus. The emancipation from a generalizing principle which manifests itself in the Aristotelian *pros hen*-relationship refers at the same time — as Aristotle himself indicates — to the process of the replacement of the generic structure by *proteron-hysteron*-gradations in the metaphysics of the Academy. According to the academic theory of gradations, as can be seen in the Aristotelian lectures *Eth. Nic.* A 4, 1096 a 17 ff. (further documentation in Krämer, p. 432, n. 98) through the example of the quantifying (mathematicizing) series of dimensions (number-line-surface-body), the succession of *proteron-hysteron* has the character of a succession of members of a series proceeding from the simpler, less determinate, from the element (*stoicheion*) to the composite, derived, and complex. "Universality" or better, the equivalent of universality (if this concept should be reserved for the abstract genus) can be defined within this "elementary ontology" as the precedence (*proteron*) and priority (with respect to being and knowledge) of the simple as a part within a series. This "simple" is something "which, as an immanent principle, is constitutively inherent (*enhyparchei*) in the complex." (*loc. cit.*, p. 352). According to Krämer Aristotle is referring to this doctrine, which Plato himself evolved in his lectures on the good, when he develops an opposing position in his critique of the doctrine of the ideas. In giving up this quantifying process Aristotle takes over the fundamental notion, according to which there is no universal standing *beside* the particular, but he transforms this notion, through his reference to the directedness (*Gerichtetheit*) of the structure of the series, to the

For Aristotle, however, this self-same One is not some sort of supra-ordinate universal; instead — and this is decisive — it is itself one of the manifold meanings. Everything healthy is related in some way, but each in a different way, to the particular condition of the body deserving of that predicate. Similarly, everything medical is related to the science of medicine. Thus the guarantor of the unity of the area of inquiry is in each case one distinctive meaning, and the relationship to this one distinctive meaning, a relationship different in each case, represents the particular sense of all the other meanings. Thus, that which is healthy in a medicinal herb is its specific relationship to a healthy bodily condition, namely, that it is conducive to it or capable of producing or preserving it. In relation to the other meanings this one meaning thus has the character of a determining factor. It is this one meaning which gives each of them their own particular meaning. Health is the determining factor of or the reason for the healthiness of a skin color or for the medicinal quality of an herb.

Because of the unity insured by this determining factor, a single and clearly circumscribed science is possible in the case of *pros hen*-manifolds as well. Therefore, it is no coincidence that the two manifolds of meaning selected as examples by Aristotle both concern a particular science, namely, the science of medicine. The unity of each particular scientific field receives its inner structure from the relatedness of all particular meanings to the one meaning among them which is normative.

We speak of "being" as also having different meanings. When we say of something, "it is..." we imply a particular size, location, quality, a condition, a relationship and so forth. But here too there is one meaning to which all others are related. Because of their relationship to this one meaning, a relationship different in each case, there can be different ways in which something can be "being" and thus different ways of saying "it is..." Aristotle sees the primary meaning in *ousia*, that is, that sense of "being" as something self-sufficient (*Selbständiges*), existing by itself (*Fürsichbestehendes*), for example, in the sense of "is"

---

pros hen-relationship, which insures the unity of the science of being by the very turning to the *kath'hekaston*.

Thus Aristotle's opposing position should not be understood primarily as a deviation from the philosophy of the academy, but rather as an option for one of the two ways of philosophizing within the Old Academy which compete with one another as elementarizing and generalizing forms of thinking. In the development of the doctrine of the academy the Aristotelian ontology appears as the "last consequence and conclusive result of an elementarizing reorganization of the generic structure" (*loc. cit.*, p. 353).

in the predication "this is a house." Thus we can say only of something big that it *is* big; its being big is related to *something which* is big, to a self-sufficient being of which size — or quality or relation and so forth — can be predicated, that is, to an *ousia*.

Thus, in the interrelated whole of the manifold meanings of "*on*," *ousia* assumes the role played by bodily health and the science of medicine. The various ways or senses of "being" — as Aristotle would say, the various categories[4] — are all related to one of them which is primary and normative, that is, to *ousia*. They are dependent upon *ousia* for their meaning.[5] The primacy peculiar to *ousia* is precisely a consequence of this, for "of the other categories, none can exist independently, only *ousia*." [6] Consequently only *ousia* has the sense of "simple being, as such" (*haples on*), whereas the others can be called being only "in some way" (*pos*), that is, mediated by their dependence upon *ousia*.

Those categories which are not self-sufficient depend upon *ousia* for their meaning. Their meaning is determined by it: *ousia* is the determining factor within the manifold meanings of *on*. For this reason Aristotle can also call *ousia* a "ground," *arche*: "Thus *on* is said in many ways, but each (of its meanings is) related to one ground." [7] *Ousia* is a ground in the sense that it bestows a particular "meaning of being" upon each of the other categories. As such a ground, *ousia* is called "primary";[8] it is primary with regard to the *logos* (concept), to *gnosis* (cognition) and to *chronos* (time).[9]

The meaning of "being" understood as *ousia* signifies, as we have seen, self-sufficient   existence-by-itself,   that   which   has   traditionally   been

---

[4] More precisely, two divisions of "being" (*seiend*) are to be found in Aristotle. On one hand *on* is above all something four-fold; it can be spoken of in the way of *on kata symbebekos*, of *on hos alethes e pseudos*, of *schemata tes kategorias* and of *dynamei or energeiai* (*Meta.* E 2, 1026 a 33 ff.). On the other hand, one of these ways signifies the *pros hen*-manifold mentioned above. The categorial *on* exhibits ten different ways of meaning of which *ousia* is the primary and normative one. In our context it is this manifold which is our main concern.

[5] *Meta.* Γ 2, 1003 b 16 f. ...ἐξ οὗ τὰ ἄλλα ἤρτηται, καὶ δι' ὃ λέγονται. Ross translates : "...on which the other things depend, and in virtue of which they get their names."

[6] *Meta.* Z 1, 1028 a 33 f. τῶν μὲν γὰρ ἄλλων κατηγορημάτων οὐθὲν χωριστόν, αὕτη δὲ μόνη.

[7] *Meta.* Γ 2, 1003 b 5 f. οὕτω δὲ καὶ τὸ ὂν λέγεται πολλαχῶς μὲν ἀλλ' ἅπαν πρὸς μίαν ἀρχήν. Ross translates : "So, too, there are many senses in which a thing is said to be, but all refer to one starting-point."

[8] Cf., *ibid.*, b 16 ff.

[9] *Meta.* Z 1, 1028 a 32 f. ...ἡ οὐσία πρῶτον, καὶ λόγῳ καὶ γνώσει καὶ χρόνῳ.

called "substance." This substance is the determining factor in the manifold senses of the "ways to be." At the same time, however, it is the
determining factor in each individual being, in the individual substances.
It determines the way in which everything which *is* a self-sufficient being
is. *Ousia* does not perform this determining-constituting function
as a transcendental principle, however. If one wishes to use this modern
set of concepts at all, then one could validly say that the Aristotelian
ousia is something like an immanent principle of organization. Substance
in this sense — perhaps we should speak instead of "substantiality"
or "essence" — is inherent in each particular thing as its fundamental
constitution: it lets it be as an *ousia*.

Being — as the meaning of the participle being [10] — necessarily
emerges for Aristotle in a comprehensive sense as *ousia*, as essence
(*Wesen*). Aristotle expresses this very clearly when he writes: "And
indeed the question which was asked of old, which is asked now and
always and which always remains open is the question: What is the *on*?
And that is just the question: What is *ousia*?" [11]

Defining the question of "being," of "ontology," as the question
of the self-sufficient, separated and simple being, as the question of
"ousiology," could be understood as a restriction, as an imposition
of barriers upon the human desire to know. By defining the question
in this way does Aristotle teach that man can never attain adequate
knowledge of the meaning of "being" (*seiend*), that everything which
man can hope to grasp is merely the meaning of *ousia* and of the other
categories? Did he thus mark the boundaries which man can approach
but never cross?

Aristotle had no such demarcation in mind. The unique characteristic
of Aristotle's ontology is that it *is* ousiology; for Aristotle *ousia* does not
signify a restriction over against the *on*. On the contrary, in *ousia* the
on itself becomes conceivable in its normative way. Thus, if it appears

---

[10] Here, with the word "Being" (*Sein*, as an infinitive) we depart from Aristotelian
terminology and adopt a concept from modern ontology in order to distinguish
metalinguistically that which appears in Aristotle as "*to on*." In this sense *to on* means
being (as a participle), its sense, its meaning, as, for example, in the sentence *to on
legetai pollachos*. Taken only linguistically, on the other hand, *to on* must be rendered
with "the being" (*das Seiende*). H. Boeder: "Weshalb Sein des Seienden?" *Philosophisches Jahrbuch*, 78. Jg. 1971, 1. Hbd., S. 111-133, has persuasively shown how
"Being" (*Sein*) cannot be spoken of until Plotinus and subsequent philosophy.

[11] *Meta.* Z 1, 1028 b 2-4. καὶ δὴ καὶ τὸ πάλαι τε καὶ νῦν καὶ ἀεὶ ζητούμενον καὶ ἀεὶ
ἀπορούμενον, τί τὸ ὄν, τοῦτό ἐστι τίς ἡ οὐσία; cf. on this point, by the author: *Heidegger
und die Tradition*, Stuttgart, 1961, p. 11.

that Aristotle first awakens an expectation with his apodictic assertion in the first chapter of *Meta*. Gamma: "There is a science which contemplates *on hei on*," but then thwarts this expectation by meeting it only in the sense of a science of *ousia*, nevertheless, according to Aristotle's own intention, this is hardly just an "only." On the contrary, this is the sole adequate way of fulfilling the peculiar meaning of *on*, insofar as it is *ousia*, the ground of being and meaning for all other categories as well as the determining ground for every concrete substantial being.

We have seen that the existence of one normative meaning among the diverse meanings of a *pros hen*-manifold is a necessary condition, if there is to be a unified science of the area of inquiry indicated by this manifold. This holds as well for the science concerned with the manifold *on*, the science of *on hei on*. In a primary and normative way, this science is concerned with the primary and normative *on*, *ousia*. Insofar as *ousia* is "being" (as a participle, i.e., *seiend*) in a "simple" sense, the science of being as being has to address itself above all to *ousia*: *ontology necessarily emerges as ousiology*.

To be sure, the doctrine of *ousia* still involves a diversity. According to *Meta*. Gamma 2, particularly 1004 a 2-9, there are as many "divisions of philosophy" as there are kinds of substance.[12] According to *Meta*. Lambda 1,[13] the sensible transitory *ousia*, the sensible eternal *ousia*, and finally, the nonsensible unmoved *ousia* can be regarded as kinds of substance. However, like the diverse kinds of *on*, these diverse kinds of *ousia* are not unrelated to one another; they are directed toward the normative, primary *ousia* among them, the *prote ousia*. In Part Three we shall deal with the relation of the question of this first and fundamental *ousia* (the question of theology) to the theory of being as being.

Aristotle unfolds his doctrine of *ousia* as such particularly in Books Zeta, Eta, and Theta of the *Metaphysics*. What is found there, however, is not a unified system of thoughts; Aristotle approaches the problem of defining *ousia* from diverse vantage points. Nonetheless, for an interpretation which seeks to follow Aristotle's argument one must always keep in mind that all the various definitions and attempts at definition

---

[12] καὶ τοσαῦτα μέρη φιλοσοφίας ἔστιν ὅσαιπερ αἱ οὐσίαι. (1004 a 2-3); cf. on this point Hans Wagner's interpretation: "Zum Problem des aristotelischen Metaphysikbegriffs," *Phil. Rundschau*, 1959, p. 144.

[13] 1069 a 30 - b 2.

pursue the same goal: the unfolding of the question of *on hei on* as the question of *ousia*.

Nevertheless, other ways of pursuing the question of *on* as such can also be found in Aristotle, if only in incipient stages, and, in principle, still presupposing that primary approach. For example, beginning with the insight developed in *Meta*. Gamma 2[14] that the meaning of "being" (as a participle, i.e., *seiend*) and the meaning of "one" are identical or convertible, Aristotle seeks such general determinations of Being as identity, diversity, similarity, unity, plurality and so on. This inquiry is found in book Iota of the *Metaphysics*.[15] The aspect of the Aristotelian doctrine of being developed there leads to the medieval interpretation of "ontology" as a doctrine of *transcendentalia*.

Yet another branch of the Aristotelian ontology should be briefly mentioned. It is the doctrine of axiomata (see above, p. 12). Aristotle explicitly shows that axiomata are a part of "ousiology."[16] Therefore they have not so much a logical as primarily an ontological sense for him. He treats of them in *Meta*. Gamma 3 ff. The main object of this doctrine is the law of contradiction.

The doctrine of fundamental determinations of *on* and *hen* developed particularly in book Iota, as well as the inquiry into the law of contradiction and into the other principles already make use of the fundamental determinations of *ousia*. In the discussions of the One as well as in those of the law of contradiction, ousiology in the narrow sense of an inquiry into the principles and definitions of *ousia* is presupposed (although not temporally presupposed, that is, as far as the sequence of the books is concerned). This can be documented especially for the doctrines of the categories, of definition and of form. Therefore, in what follows we shall limit ourselves to that aspect of Aristotle's ontology which, for an introduction into Aristotelian thought, can be regarded as its genuine core, that is, his ousiology as we find it developed, particularly in Books Zeta, Eta and Theta.

The first path the philosopher has to take to bring into view the essential constitution of any particular being consists in characterizing the *ousia* as that which underlies a thing[h], the *hypokeimenon*. What does Aristotle mean by the term "that which underlies," "*substratum*"? In the third

---

[14] *Γ* 2, 1003 b 23 ff.
[15] Cf. I. Düring, *loc. cit.*, p. 593.
[16] Cf. *Meta*. *Γ* 3, 1005 a 19 ff.

chapter of *Meta*. Zeta we read: "Now that which underlies a thing is that of which everything else is predicated, but it itself cannot be predicated of anything else." [17] In a predication, the *hypokeimenon*, that which underlies a thing, is the grammatical subject [18] of the sentence. The predicates are what are either denied or ascribed to the subjects, that is, in a judgement, they are either connected with it or separated from it through *synthesis* or *dihairesis*. As *hypokeimenon*, the *ousia* is that which underlies every judgement or predication.

Ousia qua *hypokeimenon*, however, is not only a grammatical category. The grammatical relationship in a predication reflects at the same time an ontological relationship.[19] In what way, then, is *ousia* the substrate of these changing determinations? There is good reason to define *ousia* as matter, as *hyle*, for matter is that which remains the same while form

---

[17] 1028 b 36 f. τὸ δ' ὑποκείμενόν ἐστι καθ' οὗ τὰ ἄλλα λέγεται, ἐκεῖνο δὲ αὐτὸ μηκέτι κατ' ἄλλου.

[18] Throughout Scholastic philosophy up to Descartes the translation of *hypokeimenon* was *sub-iectum* (also *substratum*) and thus connoted "object," substance. Not until after Descartes — although decisively determined by him already — did the change in the concept of subject take place, to the subjective, to "I" as the sole subject, a change which, aside from grammatical-logical terminology, has become altogether predominant in German as in English. (In Ross' translations, the reader will find the rendering *substratum* and subject. The author's German translation is *"das Zugrundeliegende"*; the reader will find slightly varying translations of this term, each one, however, indicated by a raised [h]. — *Tr*.)

[19] It should be mentioned here that Wolfgang Wieland in his book *"Die Aristotelische Physik. Untersuchungen über die Grundlegung der Naturwissenschaft und die sprachlichen Bedingungen der Prinzipienforschung bei Aristoteles"* (Göttingen, 1962), represents a different point of view on the relationship between language and being. According to Wieland, fundamental Aristotelian concepts have no sense beyond expressing "what we actually mean, when we speak of things in this way or that" (142). These principles are not "metaphysical entities" (187), but "functional or reflectional concepts" culled from language. Thus, for example, analyses of the structure of a predication do not reveal the structure of the things themselves; instead, they only serve as a guide to those "differentiating features" with "which we endeavor to think of things and what occurs with them" (186).

Wieland is certainly correct in emphasizing that Aristotle "does not posit a fundamental separation between language and things" (146). But that the ontological realm is not a realm outside of language does not mean, inversely, that ontological principles can be interpreted as being solely of a linguistic character, all the more if this linguistic aspect is understood in the modern way as something subjective, if the concepts formulated in language are to be solely "topoi" (cf. p. 202 ff.) and "viewpoints for classification."

Critical discussions of Wieland's thesis can be found in: Ernst Tugendhat, review in *Gnomon* 36 (1963), p. 543-555, and Hans Wagner: Einleitung zum *Kommentar der Physikvorlesung*. Darmstadt, 1967, p. 337-360; cf. also Klaus Oehler: *Ein Mensch zeugt einen Menschen. Über den Mißbrauch der Sprachanalyse in der Aristoteles-Forschung*. Frankfurt/M., 1963.

changes, that which now assumes one quality, now another. Moreover, matter is, without a doubt, the ultimate substrate of all determinations, whereas it itself cannot be a predicate determination. In the third chapter of *Meta*. Zeta, Aristotle himself dealt with the possibility of conceiving of *ousia* as *hypokeimenon*, as *hyle*. If one formulates the problem in this way, that is, if one defines *ousia* as *hypokeimenon*, the latter as the primary *hypokeimenon*, and this, in turn, as *hyle*, one encounters insuperable difficulties.[20] That which primarily underlies a thing[h] (*hyle*) has to be devoid of any determinations. If it were determined (defined), then one could distinguish between that which determines and that which is determined. Pure *hyle* is that which is wholly indeterminate.[21] Thus *ousia* would be pure materiality. That, however, is impossible. Why? Aristotle answers: "For both separatedness (*to choriston*) and thisness appear to belong chiefly to the essential being (*ousia*); therefore form and 'that made of both' (i.e., form and matter) would be the essential being (*ousia*) rather than matter." [22] Thus, *hyle* cannot be *ousia* because the essential being (*ousia*) is self-sufficient, a "this," in that, limited by its form, its appearance (*eidos*), it is raised above and set off from limitlessness.

But if *ousia* as *hypokeimenon* is not understood in the sense of indeterminate matter underlying every form, what is the meaning of the definition of *ousia* as that which underlies something[h]? In all determinations in which a being — however it might be constituted — is grasped, *ousia* is that which appears, or better, that which makes itself appear. Quality and quantity, spatial and temporal being are each being in *ousia*; they presuppose the *ousia* as something underlying[h]. *Ousia* is the determining ground of all those determinations which can be predicated of it, that is, of all the remaining categories. It is the first, the primary category, and this primary means precisely that *ousia* is that which underlies[h] all predication (*kategorein*).

To make this somewhat clearer: the other categories, such as a determination of quality — for example, the quality "educated" —

----

[20] On the question of the "inadequacy of the concept of essence as that which underlies something[h]" cf. R. Boehm: *Das Grundlegende und das Wesentliche*, Den Haag, 1963.

[21] *Meta*. Z 3, 1029 a 20 f.

[22] *Ibid.*, 1029 a 27-30 καὶ γὰρ τὸ χωριστὸν καὶ τὸ τόδε τι ὑπάρχειν δοκεῖ μάλιστα τῇ οὐσίᾳ, διὸ τὸ εἶδος καὶ τὸ ἐξ ἀμφοῖν οὐσία δόξειεν ἂν εἶναι μᾶλλον τῆς ὕλης. Ross translates: "For both separability and 'thisness' are thought to belong chiefly to substance. And so form and the compound of form and matter would be thought to be substance, rather than matter."

are indebted for their factual existence solely to a being in the sense of
the primary category, in the sense of an *ousia* in which they occur. The
quality of being educated itself is only "something added," something
"coincidental," a *symbebekos, accidens*. On the other hand, it is inherent
to the fundamental character of *ousia* that it is "in" itself, not "in"
something else, by itself and not with something else. However, it
is not "in and by itself" to such a degree that it is unconnected to the
other categories, or excludes them altogether; rather, that it underlies[h]
them means that it is able to receive other determinations.

Initially, that is, with regard to its mere presence, that which receives
on the one hand, and the added or coincidental determinations on the
other, are not at all separate from one another. In the *Categories*,
Aristotle distinguishes between a primary and secondary *ousia*. He
characterizes the primary *ousia* as that which "is neither predicated of
something underlying[h] nor present in something underlying." [23] As
examples he cites "this man" and "this horse." Here the primary *ousia*
is thus present, individual concrete being. Noetic thinking apprehends
— as we have seen earlier (see above, p. 6) — this individual being
in the indivisible essence forming it into a whole. Such a unity is not
yet divided into an underlying essence — such as Man — and the
manifold qualities inhering in it — such as educated, blond, tall, and
so forth. Differentiation does not come about until the moment when
that thinking or contemplating which initially just takes simple cognizance
of something makes the transition to a specifying predication, to an
explicit ascription or denial of particular determinations in a judgement
of dianoetic thinking.

However, *ousia* itself can also be ascribed to something in this way.
It need not function only as a subject; it is also capable of functioning
in a predication as the predicate itself, as, for instance, in the sentence:
"This is a house." Predications which ascribe or deny do not only answer
questions of "where?, when?, how much?, how large?" and so on,
but also the question "what?" Such a what-question seeks a definition,
for example: "What is Man?"

If the answer to a what-question is not to be a mere tautology then
such an answer must display the predicates, the underlying being in

---

[23] *Cat.* 5, 2 a 12 f. ...ἢ μήτε καθ' ὑποκειμένου τινὸς λέγεται μήτε ἐν ὑποκειμένῳ τινί
ἐστιν. E. M. Edgehill (ed. Ross) translates: "...that which is neither predicable of a
subject nor present in a subject."

itself, that is, of its essence. The what-question concerns those determinations which, in the *Categories*, are called the secondary *ousiai*,
"in which, as species, the primary *ousiai* are present." [24] The *ousia*
underlying[h] the essential determination of a thing is not so much a
separate, self-sufficient individual — "this man" — but, rather, that
which characterizes and forms that individual as such a thing — "Man"
or "living thing." We shall return later to this sense of *ousia*, which
can be summarized in the word *eidos*; first, however, we shall consider
the aim of an essential definition, the answer to a what-question, that is,
the definition.

A definition articulates the essential aspects of the simple essence of
a self-sufficient being. The question "what is...?" "*ti esti...?*," already
recognizes the Being of a particular individual in what it already was
(*ti en einai*). Taking this, what was already seen, as its point of
departure, the answer analyzes it into the parts which make up the
definition of essence. For Aristotle, the essence itself is indeed a unity,
adihaireton, *asyntheton*, which shows itself as something indivisible
in *noesis*, for in *noesis* it becomes present (see above, p. 8). Nevertheless,
this does not exclude the possibility that it can be analyzed into parts
by the process of dianoetic definition.

But what kind of "parts" are these which make up the essence of a
being? Here again it is a question of a relationship of determinations,
that is, a universal which underlies the thing[h] is distinguished by determinations ascribed to it until it is finally identified as this particular
being. The differentiation occurs by limitation: for example, the realm
"living things," still very general, is differentiated more closely by
being divided into those living things which dwell upon land and those
which dwell in the water. Every subordinate realm arrived at in this way
is, in turn, subdivided again, until one arrives at the final characteristics
which distinguish a particular living thing from all other living things.
The universal underlying[h] the differentiating definition is the genus
to which a particular being belongs. The process of thought leading
to a definition begins with the genus and breaks it down into species

---

[24] *Ibid.*, a 14 f. ...ἐν οἷς εἴδεσιν αἱ πρώτως οὐσίαι λεγόμεναι ὑπάρχουσιν. E. M. Edgehill
(ed. Ross) translates: "But in a secondary sense those things are called substances
within which, as species, the primary substances are included." Thus the "secondary
ousiai" are the *eide* in which the *ousiai*, in the primary sense, are present, or the *gene*
of these *eide*. Thus, here this man is present in the species "Man" and in the genus
"living things." "Man" and "living things" are thus *ousiai* in the secondary sense
(*op. cit.*, 2 a 14).

by means of specific differences. If the latter are limited still further, thinking will finally reach the "last species," the *infima species*. This is the essence of the individual sought in the what-question and articulated in the definition. The elements of this articulation, the "parts" mentioned above, are thus not simply components, one next to another, for then they would not be capable of being a One (Unity), that is, of being the unified What of the essence sought in an essential determination. Instead, the "parts" combine into that unity of essence, in that one part is the differentiating determination of the other, of that which underlies it[h]. The particular way in which Aristotle attempts to solve the problem of understanding the unity of Being by means of its essential aspects will concern us more closely below.[25]

As Aristotle recognized himself, his definitional approach to the determination of *ousia* leads, however, to certain difficulties. He writes: "But when it comes to the concrete whole, for example, this circle, that is a particular, individual circle, be it perceptible or intelligible...of these there is no definition; they are known only by means of *noesis* (intuitive apprehension) or *aisthesis* (perception)..." [26] Aristotle realizes that only universals can be attained through definition as, for example, the essential determination of man as a "biped living thing." [27] The particular individual cognized noetically or perceptually (by *aisthesis*) includes something which essentially escapes all general determination: *hyle*. And likewise, the cognition of the essence of a particular individual, of a "this," would also have to include the particular *hyle*, not just the *eidos*. Although Aristotle sees that it is possible to define the *eidos* "concavity," he is helpless when confronted with the question of how one should define "snubnosedness" (*simotes*), even though it is the essence of a particular, real nose.[28] Similarly, one *can* indeed define man, if one regards only his *eidos* as appearance and form. But does the definition really touch the essence of "this" man as an individual (*hekaston*)?

---

[25] Cf. below, p. 36 ff. on *dynamis* and *energeia*.

[26] *Meta.* Z 10, 1036 a 2-6: τοῦ δὲ συνόλου ἤδη, οἷον κύκλου τουδὶ καὶ τῶν καθ' ἔκαστά τινος ἢ αἰσθητοῦ ἢ νοητοῦ...τούτων δὲ οὐκ ἔστιν ὁρισμός, ἀλλὰ μετὰ νοήσεως ἢ αἰσθήσεως γνωρίζονται. The translation adopts Ross' version, with some changes.

[27] The definition of man used most often in Aristotle's metaphysical treatises is "biped living thing." As opposed to the definitions — whose meanings are more relevant — such as "*zoon logon politikon*" this definition clearly expresses the connection between the logical doctrine of definition and the biological division of the realm of living things. Cf. on this point: K. Oehler, *op. cit.*

[28] Cf. *Meta.* E 1, 1025 b 30 ff.; Z 11, 1037 a 30 ff.

Aristotle sees that definitional thinking, and perhaps dianoetical thinking and its truth, is not capable of fully articulating noetic thinking and its truth. The philosophy of our century has sensed in various ways an inadequacy about the limits of dianoetic thinking, and because of this, has set out on the pathway to think anew the "essence" of essence (das "Wesen" des Wesens). To be sure, philosophy has occasionally seen itself compelled to surrender the character of philosophy as *theoria* in the sense of noetic-dianoetic contemplation. It has drawn closer to "praxis" or has become altogether combined with praxis, which — like Aristotelian *phronesis* — is always concerned with the individual life situation. The trends of contemporary philosophy have thus entered a danger zone, since the position philosophy once occupied as the "head" of the sciences, as the inquiry into the supreme and most venerable objects is being relinquished.

But let us return to Aristotle. Although the process of definition is not able to articulate the concrete being in its individuality, its own peculiar significance lies, conversely, in its very universality. Traditional scientific thinking essentially originating with Aristotle, necessarily requires definitions which grasp the being to be cognized with consistency and general validity. The definitional determination of *ousia* may indeed be incapable of exhausting its essence, but this process signifies the necessary step from mere contemplation of the *ti en einai* to articulate, scientific comprehension.

But what about the essence itself? The name for "what" or essence [29] articulated in definition — as we just saw, in scientific universality — is *ti en einai* or *eidos*. Within the context of this book it is not our purpose to clarify the still controversial question of how the expression "*to*

---

[29] On the Scholastic understanding of essence, see, for example, Thomas of Aquinas' first work, *De ente et essentia*. In Chapter One we read: "Et quia illud, per quod res constituitur in proprio genere vel specie, est hoc quod significatur per definitionem indicantem quid est res, inde est quod nomen essentiae a philosophis in nomen quidditatis mutatur. Et hoc quod PHILOSOPHUS frequenter nominat quod quid erat esse id est hoc, per quod aliquid habet esse quid." (Thomas v. Aquin: *Über das Sein und das Wesen*, deutsch-lat. Ausgabe üb. und erl. v. R. Allers, Wissenschaftliche Buchgemeinschaft, Tübingen o.J., p. 17). In his postscript R. Allers holds: "According to the doctrine of Aquinas, the essence is not initially related to a single being-thus-there-and-now (*ein einzelnes Da-jetzt-so-Seiendes*) into which matter has penetrated in an all-round determinate way; for matter is comprised in the essence not as a concrete-this-there, that is, as something designated in quantity (*materia designata quantitate*), but only in a general, as a correlate to form. Hence, a definition of Man is possible, but not of a concrete, individual man. Matter, however, enters only the essence of physical things in the way indicated. The intelligible substances are devoid of matter (thus: *substantiae separatae*)" (p. 74).

ti en einai," formulated by Aristotle can be more precisely understood grammatically,[30] particularly as concerns the imperfect "*en.*" It remains true, however, that this determination attempts to provide the first answer to the "what-is-question" (*ti esti*) which the philosopher poses to that which appears to him, whereas the definition is then a universal explication of the answer to the *ti-esti*-question posed about an individual being. Explicitly or implicitly the particular being whose *ti en einai* is in the question is included in the concept of "*ti en einai*," for example, *to ti en anthropo einai* ("what is was for Man to be," that is, the essence of Man).[31] The *ti en einai* is the "what" determination of each individual being. For Aristotle this determination is essentially inherent in that which renders a being visible, in that which forms it into this particular being, in its *eidos*. *Eidos* is what appears in an *eidenai*, in knowledge achieved by seeing, not seeing by perception, but that "mental" seeing characterized more precisely above (see above, p. 6). For this reason, with regard to one of its essential aspects *eidos* can be translated with "appearance." It is the appearance a "what," such as a house, a table or a living thing presents, the appearance of a particular "shape" (*morphe*). In this sense the artist envisions the *eidos* of what he intends to create. In his mind's eye he sees the appearance of a "what," of a shape.

The appearance of a being as it shows itself connects it at the same time with all being of the same appearance. Thus *eidos* also has the meaning "species." The species of the being grasped in a definition indicates the appearance common to this being and to others of like species.

That *ousia* is *eidos*, appearance, however, means above all — and this is the meaning of the term most important for the history of its effect on philosophy — that it is the "form" in the sense of an active process of formation. In the realm of transient being composed of form and matter, *eidos* and *hyle*, the *eidos* forms the *hyle* into a concrete individual, into a *synholon*. *Hyle*, as we have seen (see above, p. 22 f.), signifies that which in itself is indeterminate; it is that which in itself is "obscure," which can come forward as something visible only through the illuminating power of the *eidos*. For Aristotle, "matter is unknow-

---

[30] Cf. on this problematic the comprehensive and more extensive discussion by Fr. Bassenge: "*Das to heni einai to agathoi einai etc. etc., und das to ti en einai bei Aristoteles.*" In: *Philologus* 104, 1960, p. 14-47, p. 201-222, as well as the review of this treatise by E. Tugendhat. In: *Gnomon*, Vol. 33, 1961, p. 705, n. 1.

[31] The expression "*to anthropoi einai*" is used in a related way.

able in itself." [32] *Eidos* forms the matter and thus individualizes itself into a particular *synholon*. Thus the soul (*eidos*) in this body (*hyle*) is the individual Socrates. And only in relation to the *eidos* "house" are the stones "this masonry" and the timber "these beams." To be sure, it is also true conversely that without this *hyle*, without timber and stones, this house could not have come into being. But however important the *hyle* in a *synholon* may be, the *eidos* is still the decisive component in this correlation. In a wooden statue the being-a-statue given in its form is more important than the wood of which it is made. When we encounter such a work of art, we direct our attention to the form of a statue and not to its being wooden. [33]

The *eidos* is that "in relation to which" something is this particular one and not another. " 'That in relation to which' is in its primary sense the *eidos* and in a secondary sense the *hyle* of each thing." [34]

The way Aristotle defines *eidos* as intransient is of central significance for his conception of *ousia* as form. [35] Aristotle's decisive thought which was to supersede the Platonic *chorismos*, the dualism of intransient idea and transient being, is that an essence which is intransient and apart from all becoming, and in this sense "eternal" is present in concrete Being, in the transient *synholon*. For western thought it was particularly significant that Aristotle sought to posit a synthesis of Being and becoming in the realm ruled by transiency, in the realm of earthly beings, *synhola*. One of the great intellectual accomplishments in the history of philosophy is that Aristotle — unlike Plato — did not define movable, transient being, *on gignomenon*, as non-being, as *me on*, rather he saw something intransient "in" it, and thus "saved" or "delivered"

[32] *Meta.* Z 10, 1036 a 8 f. ἡ δ' ὕλη ἄγνωστος καθ' αὑτήν. We have adopted Ross' translation.

[33] As Aristotle remarks himself, this greater meaning of form is already expressed by the fact that the usual name of a thing is the same as the name of its form, cf. *Meta.* H 3, 1043 a 29 ff.

[34] *Meta.* Δ 18, 1022 a 17 f. τὸ μὲν οὖν πρώτως λεγόμενον καθ' ὃ τὸ εἶδός ἐστιν, δευτέρως δὲ ὡς ἡ ὕλη ἑκάστου ... Ross translates: "that in virtue of which..."

[35] One consequence of this definition became problem-historically decisive : if there is no change in the essence, then there can be nothing which is really new, which has never been before. This essential result of the fundamental trait of the self-sameness and the eternity of *ousia* was decisive for subsequent philosophy and entangled it in great difficulties when the advent of something new was declared; it brought every attempt at "historical" or "epochal" thinking into contradiction with itself; it left certain findings in the natural sciences unexplained, such as the discovery of the origin of "new species" and mutations and it obstructed, again and again, any philosophical access to the secret of a work of art which creates something totally new.

the transient individual into the eternal actuality of Being of a none-theless movable order.

The *eidos* neither comes or goes. As opposed to the being whose *eidos* it is, it is not subject to coming-into-being,[36] *genesis*, or passing away, *phthora*.[37] It would be absurd to assume that an artist who, for example, produces a bronze ball first produces the form of roundness itself as well; that would mean that the process of producing something would never come to an end, since the form would have to be produced from something else, this something in turn from something else, and so on. Thus, according to Aristotle, the essence "house," for example, is also intransient and apart from all becoming. When a house is built, this does not signify the origin of the *eidos* house; instead, the appearance and form (*eidos*) already present in the "soul" of the master-builder, that which makes a house a house, is impressed upon the building materials. "A house is always produced only from a house, health always only from health" or, in general, "anything at all only from something of the same name." [38]

In the *Physics*,[39] in his treatise on the essence of time, Aristotle distinguishes the eternity of *onta*, perpetual being, from the realm of "beings-in-time"; eternal beings are not "contained by time" nor is their Being "measured by time." [40] The meaning of eternity is determined for *ousia* by its being "non-temporal" or "extra-temporal." As *eidos*, *ousia* does not succumb to the destructive power of time, nor can it be measured by means of the enumeration of a movement only in space.[41] In particular, *ousia* ought not be grasped from the standpoint of

---

[36] *Meta. Λ* 3, 1070 a 15; cf. also *Meta.* Z 8, 1033 b 5-19; H 3, 1043 b 17; Θ 10, 1051 b 29 f.; *Λ* 3, 1069 b 35 ff.

[37] It should be remarked that in spite of the *ousia*'s traits of self-sameness and of being eternal, the problem of the coming-into-being of an essence *qua synholon* (*genesis haplos*) still existed for Aristotle. For him, the genuine problem of *genesis* lay in the coming-into-being or into-essence of a man, an animal, a thing, or a work of art. In this occurrence, the *eidos*, the "whither" of this movement and the latter's privative form, the *steresis*, or the "whence" of this movement, mesh with one another. Together with the *hypokeimenon*, these interrelated factors form the structure of the process of *genesis* (cf. *Phys.* A 5-7), so that the Aristotelian ideal of a self-maintaining — although movable — order is in no way endangered by the possibility of such "changes."

[38] Cf. *Meta.* Z 9, 1034 a 21 ff. Ross translates: "...every product of art is produced from a thing which shares its name..."

[39] *Phys. Δ* 10, 217 b 29 ff.

[40] *Phys. Δ* 12, 221 b 3-7. Translations by Hardie and Gaye, in the Ross edition.

[41] As is well known, this is the Aristotelian definition of time; cf. *Phys. Δ* 11, 219 b 1 f.; τοῦτο γάρ ἐστιν ὁ χρόνος, ἀριθμὸς κινήσεως κατὰ τὸ πρότερον καὶ ὕστερον.

the now, of the present. In the realm of natural beings, Aristotle considers
the intransiency of the *eidos* to be guaranteed because the essence "Man"
remains beyond all becoming and passing away throughout the chain of
generations and births, even though the individual man "comes into" his
matter and passes away, is born and dies. Just as the *eidos* of anything
to be produced by technical means is already pre-given in the productive
knowledge of its producer and remains there, the *eidos* of any natural
being is pre-given in its producer. Thus the eternity of the *ousia* emerges
here as the eternity of the species.[42]

It is inherent in the intransiency of the *eidos* that, as the "indwelling
form" it insures that the *synholon* remain the *same*, despite the vicissitudes
of change occurring to it. The *ousia* as *eidos* grants a being self-sameness.
In keeping with his quest for "the one and the many" (*hen kai polla*),
Plato defined self-sameness (*tautotes*) by means of a *contrast* to the
many. For Aristotle, on the other hand, it is defined by means of a
relation to the many, the accidentally concomitant beings, the *sym-
bebekota*. Thus, for example, the qualitative determinations of a being
can change; this is the case with change in its narrower sense,[43] with
alloiosis. For example, an "uneducated" man becomes an "educated"
man. The change (*metabole*) of an accidental quality, the quality of
being uneducated, into another quality, the quality of being educated,
takes place in such a way that the one perishes as the other comes
into being. This change occurs in something which nevertheless remains
self-same, in something abiding, the *synholon*, "this man." "This
man" persists as such. He endures as the self-same one in his relationship to his changing qualities.[44] Socrates remains the self-same one,
whether he be sitting or walking, young or old. The enduring self-
same one is the self-sufficient individual. But what guarantees, so to
speak, this individual its identity is the particular essence in which it is
present, its *ousia* in the sense of its essential form, its *eidos*. The qualitative change in the determinations of a being is not capable of influen-
cing the being itself in its *eidos*. In fact, the *eidos* lends order to the
"unself-same" changing determinations as well, by prescribing the

Ross edition: "For time is just this — number of motion in respect of 'before' and
'after'."

[42] Cf. on this problematic the essay by K. Oehler: *Ein Mensch zeugt einen Menschen*,
Frankfurt/Main, p. 37 ff.

[43] As opposed to change in the broader sense, which includes change of place as
well as increase and decrease.

[44] Cf. *Phys.* A 7, 190 a 13 ff.

scope of the determinations or qualities which can appear in a being. Thus, a man can change from being uneducated to being educated, but never — as if he were the leaf of a plant — from being green to being yellow.

Thus the change of a being takes place as a change of its determinations or qualities, more precisely, as the change, or "conversion" of one determination into its opposite. To this extent, each of them represents the absence of its opposite; conversely, every determination — such as being educated — arises out of its opposite, or its privation (*steresis*) — such as being uneducated.

The change of contrasting determinations is made possible, however, by that alone which underlies[h] both, the *ousia* as *hypokeimenon* which endures throughout its ever-changing determinations as the self-same one. The self-sameness of the *ousia* is the self-sameness of the appearance (*eidos*) which presents itself throughout all changes always in the same way.

It may have become clear that the definition of *ousia* as the self-sameness of an enduring self is an expansion upon what was said above concerning *ousia* as that which underlies[h] all the categorical determinations ascribed to it. That which actually provides the ground in this being, however, is its *eidos* or *ti en einai*. This is a *haploun*, something simple, something which, in relation to categorical or other determinations, is *primary*.

In chapter 17 of *Meta*. Zeta, Aristotle treats the problem of how *ousia* can be the ground or cause not only as the one and the self-same throughout all the constantly changing accidental determinations, but moreover as the ground or cause uniting that split articulated in the definition which forms its essence.

The last chapter of Book Zeta of the *Metaphysics* concerns *ousia* as the cause of being. Aristotle proceeds by first discussing the structure of the question itself and thus of any why-question in general. In this context he shows that the particular question concerning essence as cause is also bound up with this general structure. Precisely in this way, one sees how *ousia* can be logically defined as the "object of a question" ("*Erfragtes*").[45]

---

[45] In modern Aristotelian scholarship the difficult 17th Chapter of *Metaphysics* Z has been throughly discussed often: cf. particularly: Günter Patzig : "Die Entwicklung des Begriffes der Usia in der Metaphysik des Aristoteles." Diss. Göttingen 1950 (typewritten); Ernst Tugendhat: *Ti Kata Tinos*. Freiburg-Munich, 1958;

What is the structure of a why-question for Aristotle? Generally speaking, when one asks — *dia ti* — why something is, one is asking, "why does one thing attach to some other?" [46] The object of this inquiry must have the structure of this relationship. This is a two-fold structure in which something underlying[h], a *hypokeimenon*, is related to something else which can be ascribed to it or denied it.[47] If what is in question is to be open to a why question, then it must have such a "katallel-structure." [48] The question "why is the educated man an educated man?" can be meaningfully answered only in this way: Because being-educated is ascribed to the man, the *hypokeimenon*, as that which attaches to him. Aristotle contrasts this sort of meaningful question and answer with the "meaningless" questions which ask "why a thing is itself," as for example, in the question: "Why is Man Man?" Such a question, declares Aristotle

---

Klaus Oehler: *Die Lehre vom noetischen und dianoetischen Denken bei Platon und Aristoteles*. Munich, 1962; Rudolph Boehm: *Das Grundlegende und das Wesentliche*. The Hague 1965; Ute Guzzoni: *Grund und Allgemeinheit: Untersuchungen zum aristotelischen Verständnis der ontologischen Gründe*, Meisenheim am Glan, 1975.

[46] *Meta.* Z 17, 1041 a 11: διὰ τί ἄλλο ἄλλῳ τινὶ ὑπάρχει. We have adopted Ross' translation.

[47] 1041 a 23.

[48] We have taken the term "katallel" from Rudolph Boehm: *Das Grundlegende und das Wesentliche* (The Hague, 1965), who introduced it into German as a name for this relationship (*Verhältnismäßigkeit*) when speaking of being, deriving the term from the Aristotelian phrase ἐν τοῖς...κατ' ἀλλήλων λεγομένοις (1041 a 33). — Since Boehm's work is the most recent publication to have discussed Zeta 17 thoroughly, the central train of thought of this discussion should be briefly mentioned here. According to Boehm, in the closing chapter of *Meta.* Zeta, the tension between the two fundamental definitions of *ousia* becomes eminently apparent: on the one hand it is *hypokeimenon*, "something underlying" ("*Zugrundeliegendes*") and as such is arranged in a "relationship" ("*Verhältnismäßigkeit*"), in accordance with the "katallel way of regarding something" ("*katallele Blickweise*"); on the other hand it is *ti en einai*, "being-what-it-was" ("*Sein-was-es-war*"), a simple concept of the essence, "strict in-itself" ("*strenges An-ihm-selbst*") (189). The inquiry in Zeta 17 "aims at the essence and consequently, if the following is also otherwise an adequate concept of the essential form of the essence, at the *being-what-it-was*" (192). At the same time, however, it is inherent in the nature of an inquiry that it must always inquire first with a view to the relationship of a katallel (190), that is, of something underlying and something which attaches to it. The simple *ti en einai*, which, in any inquiry, is necessarily obvious from the first, is therefore a cause "which cannot be 'brought into question' at all" (195). Now if Aristotle still wishes — in accordance with the fundamental question of metaphysics — to inquire into the essence as cause, it follows, according to Boehm, "that as matter, the *primary* cause must be *that which underlies*[h] ("*das Zugrundeliegende*") (196). Thus, because of the nature of the inquiry, it passes over, so to speak, the simple and self-evident "Being-what-it-was", which thus "initially conceals itself" (*idem.*), and addresses itself to the essence as something underlying[h] (*Zugrundeliegendes*), and thus — with regard to the latter — to the "appearance" ("*Anblick*") which " 'mediates' to matter its whatness" (*idem.*).

bluntly, is a question about nothing.[49] He argues that such a question is meaningless because the "that" and Being must already have been present as something obvious.[50] Thus, in order to be able to ask the two-fold structured why-question, the fact that a man is present and that he is a man has to be given. This why-question is valid for every inquiry into "physical" causes for an instance of coming into being or passing away. For "we do not think we know a thing until we know the 'why' of it..." [51]

One inquires into the causes of a thing in the sense of its matter, its form and shape, the force which moves or "effects" it, or of its purpose or aim (see below, p. 38 f.).[52]

The question at hand in Zeta 17, however, is still the determination of the fundamental character of essence as such.[53] How is the "grounding" accomplished which makes this essential being, for example a man, the kind of essential being it is? For Aristotle this "grounding" as well can only be determined in the framework of a logical why-question. In a simple question — comparable to the simple question: what is Man? — what is in question, the ousia as cause, remains "the most concealed";[54] moreover, this would again amount to an inquiry into nothing.[55] In order to pose a why-question, as we have seen, one must recast the matter as a "katallel-structure"; here as well one must ask about that which attaches to what underlies a thing[h] (hypokeimenon).

In considering the question of the determination of the cause of an essential being — such as Man — where can one find the required two-fold structure? It can be only found in those fundamental determinations which constitute being and make a being this particular synholon, as a

---

[49] 1041 a 14 f. οὐδέν ἐστι ζητεῖν.

[50] 1041 a 15 δεῖ γὰρ τὸ ὅτι καὶ τὸ εἶναι ὑπάρχειν δῆλα ὄντα.

[51] Phys. B 3, 194 b 18 f. εἰδέναι δὲ οὐ πρότερον οἰόμεθα ἕκαστον πρὶν ἂν λάβωμεν τὸ διὰ τί περὶ ἕκαστον. cf. Meta. A 3, 983 a 25 f.

[52] Cf. Meta. Z 17, 1041 a 27 ff.

[53] In the treatise cited above, E. Tugendhat thoroughly presented the ontological necessity for understanding ousia as the ground of a thing. In the first three sections of his book he demonstrates in detail how Aristotle shows that something which is present-to-us (das Anwesende) "as something two-fold present in the way that a thing lying before us is present (Präsenz von Vorliegendem, ti kata tinos)" (op. cit., p. 121). In the final and most important section, he shows how Aristotle then endeavored to reduce the two-fold to a unity once again, that is, to inquire into the ground for the unity of this manifold, into the mediating factor (the meson, cf. Post. An. B 2) of the two-fold.

[54] 1041 a 32 f. λανθάνει δὲ μάλιστα.

[55] 1041 b 3 f. κοινὸν τοῦ μηθὲν ζητεῖν καὶ τοῦ ζητεῖν τι γίγνεται.

"two-fold" structure composed of *hyle* and *eidos*. The question of how the essence as the cause (*Grund*) of a man actually does "cause" must then be posed in this way: why is this body (*hyle*), with this particular form (*eidos*), a man? [56] The question now becomes, what is the cause of the matter by virtue of which it is this particular thing, for example, a house.[57] Aristotle answers: tiles and stones compose a house "because the *ti en einai* of a house is present."[58] Hence, because of this two-fold composition of *hyle* and *eidos* we come to the conclusion that the *ti en einai* is the cause in question,[59] namely, the cause of this two-fold structure of *hyle* and *eidos*. Thus, the fundamental character of the essence lies in the fact that it provides the cause of this two-fold structure; it accomplishes this, moreover, as the *ti en einai*, which can be logically defined in terms of a *horismos*, that is, ultimately through the two-fold structure of *hyle* and *eidos*.[60]

But what about the *ti en einai* itself? As we know, it is something "simple." Can the *ti en einai* in turn also be "caused?" Or by pointing out that this inquiry is bound up with the katallel structure did Aristotle want to show us that the *ti en einai* is not itself capable of being "caused"? As the unity of a thing identical with itself it is indeed something "evident" in itself which nonetheless is not apparent when one inquires into the causes for which a *synholon* comes into being or passes away. But what does Aristotle mean when he says that in the case of the "simple" an investigation (which means: like the preceding one) is impossible and that a different kind of investigation is necessary? Here we can see a reference to the "touching" of a simple essence by the intuitive understanding which we have already covered in Part One (see above, p. 6).

In Book Eta, which follows the discussion just dealt with above, Aristotle

[56] Cf. *ibid.*, b 6 f.
[57] Cf. *ibid.*, b 7.
[58] *Ibid.*, b 6 ὅτι ὑπάρχει ὃ ἦν οἰκίᾳ εἶναι. Ross translates: "Because that which was the essence of a house is present."
[59] Cf. 1041 a 28.
[60] On the understanding of the train of thought in Z 17 underlying these paragraphs cf. the interpretation of this chapter in: U. Guzzoni, *op. cit.*, p. 144-227. There, a thorough analysis of the text shows that the two-fold structure required by the why-question, of that thing whose *ousia* is supposed to be the cause of the thing, i.e., the two-fold of *hyle* and *eidos*, means the same thing as the two-fold of the terms of a definition. The *ousia* is the cause in that as the *ti en einai* — which, in the context of this question, is to be distinguished from the *eidos* — it allows the two-fold structure to exist as that single, unified thing of which it is the essence.

turns to the basic concepts, *hyle* and *eidos*, in terms of which he had previously conceived of any *synholon*. He now develops these basic concepts as *dynamis* and *energeia*, potentiality and actuality. In the interplay between *dynamis*, potentiality, and *energeia*, actuality, the process of determining an *ousia* is accomplished in such a way that these interrelated aspects express the inner movement of an essential being. By means of these concepts Aristotle is able to show how the twofold structure of *hyle* and *eidos* was actually always bridged, for *hyle* and *eidos* become "one." "Further, *hyle* exists as a potentiality, just because it can come to its form; but when it exists as an actuality, then it is in its form." [61]

A piece of gold has the potential to become a statue, although it is not yet a statue. In relation to the statue, the gold is the *hyle*, for it is the potentiality, *dynamis*, of the movement which is its generation or coming-into-being. Even in a gold statue already completed, however, the gold remains the potentiality of the statue, although no longer as the potentiality to become something else. In a certain respect, the gold is the statue itself; it is the gold-ness in the statue. The gold has now become what the *eidos* "statue" is as well. In the *synholon* statue the *eidos* is *in* the *hyle*; as the statue, *hyle* and *eidos* are the same.

But, as has been said, the ultimate *hyle* [62] and the *morphe* (that is the *eidos*) are one and the same, the one potentially and the other actually; thus it would be the same if one wanted to ask what is the cause of unity in general (*Einessein*, "being one") and what is the cause of their being one; for each thing is a unity, and the potential and the actual are somehow one.[63]

---

[61] *Meta.* Θ 8, 1050 a 15 f. Ross translates: "Further, matter exists in a potential state, just because it may come to its form; and when it exists actually, then it is in its form."

[62] ἐσχάτη ὕλη should be understood as the highest, most differentiated level in the structure of matter, where *hyle* can immediately enter into relation with a definite form. The more differentiated the concrete substance (*Wesen*), the more differentiated will be its "individual matter." This ἐσχάτη ὕλη appears, for example, as the corpse of a man from which the soul (= form) has departed (cf. *Meteor. Δ* 12, 389 b 31). The conception of a ἐσχάτη ὕλη presupposes a sequential structure of strata from *hylai* down to *prote hyle* in which the individual strata can relate in turn to one another as form and matter. Within this structure the *prote hyle*, as the lowest substrate, is void of all differentiation. It is distinct from the *hyle*-principle itself. In this lowest substrate, the *hyle* is thought of as the absolutely indeterminate (and that implies also unknowable), as pure potentiality. On these questions, see the comprehensive inquiry by Heinz Happ: *Hyle, Studien zum aristotelischen Materie-Begriff*, Berlin, 1971 (especially section 8.2).

[63] *Meta.* H 6, 1045 b 17-21 ἔστι δ', ὥσπερ εἴρηται, ἡ ἐσχάτη ὕλη καὶ ἡ μορφὴ ταὐτὸ καὶ ἕν, τὸ μὲν δυνάμει, τὸ δὲ ἐνεργείᾳ, ὥστε ὅμοιον τὸ ζητεῖν τοῦ ἑνὸς τί αἴτιον καὶ τοῦ ἓν εἶναι· ἓν γάρ τι ἕκαστον, καὶ τὸ δυνάμει καὶ τὸ ἐνεργείᾳ ἕν πώς ἐστιν.

The fact that the *hyle* and *eidos* of a being are one and the same means nothing more than that they are understood as the potentiality and actuality of a being, as the moving forces whose interplay allows the being to be the particular being that it is.

In defining *dynamis*, potentiality, Aristotle distinguishes between potentiality related to motion, "possibility" in a narrower sense, [64] and possibility in a broader sense of "potentiality." [65] With regard to the former kind of potentiality, he distinguishes in turn between the possibility to do, to be active, and the possibility to suffer, to be passive.[66]

Energeia is defined as the actualization of both of these kinds of *dynamis*, of the possibility to act and to suffer, as well as of "potentiality." Aristotle clarifies the relationship between potentiality and actuality with the following analogy: "...as that which builds is to that which is capable of building, and the waking to the sleeping, and that which is seeing to that which has its eyes shut but has sight...." [67] Aristotle continues: "Let actuality be defined by one member of this opposition and the possible by the other." [68] This definition also shows that *energeia* and *dynamis* are stages in a moving unity which together — each requiring the other — constitute the power of substantiality.

Nevertheless, within this unity, a certain priority is granted to the *energeia*; "it is clear that *energeia* is prior to potentiality." [69] Must not this statement seem paradoxical, if the potential is supposed to be the very presupposition of the actual, of the actualization of a being? Aristotle distinguishes between three ways in which something can be "prior."[70]

1. "Prior" with regard to concept, or logically "prior" (*logo*) :[71] Conceptually, an ability or disposition is grasped in terms of the actualization of this ability. The concept of building is logically (*logo*) prior to the concept of builder.

---

[64] *Meta.* Θ 1, 1046 a 1 ff.

[65] Cf. Θ 6, 1048 a 27 ff.

[66] Cf. Θ 1, 1046 a 11 ff.

[67] Θ 6, 1048 a 37 ff. ὡς τὸ οἰκοδομοῦν πρὸς τὸ οἰκοδομικόν, καὶ τὸ ἐγρηγορὸς πρὸς τὸ καθεῦδον, καὶ τὸ ὁρῶν πρὸς τὸ μῦον μὲν ὄψιν δὲ ἔχον ...

[68] *Ibid.*, 1048 b 4-6 ταύτης δὲ τῆς διαφορᾶς θάτερον μόριον ἔστω ἡ ἐνέργεια ἀφωρισμένη, θάτερον δὲ τὸ δυνατόν. Ross translates: "Let actuality be defined by one member of this antithesis, and the potential by the other."

[69] Θ 8, 1049 b 5 φανερὸν ὅτι πρότερον ἐνέργεια δυνάμεώς ἐστιν. Ross translates "potency."

[70] On the following cf.: J. Stallmach, *op. cit.*, p. 135 ff. and p. 155 ff.

[71] Commentators equate the *proteron logo* with that which "prior with regard to cognition" (*gnosei proteron*); cf. J. Stallmach, *op. cit.*, p. 143.

2. "Prior" with regard to time, or temporally "prior" (*chrono*). To be sure, in the genesis of an individual being, the potentiality, the disposition is prior to its actualization. Taking the process of becoming as whole, however, actuality must always precede potentiality temporally if there is to be any actualization at all. Thus, with regard to the genesis of an individual living being, such as man, the seed is temporally prior to the man, but temporally "prior" even to the seed is that man, who, as the "why," produces this man: "for from the potentially existing the actually existing is always produced by an actually existing thing." [72] A man produces a man, and a learned man can make another man learned. The "why" of actualization and motion (on *energeia* and *kinesis*, see below p. 43 ff.) is temporally prior.[73]

3. "Prior" with regard to *ousia*. If one considers a being's becoming as a "becoming toward being," then, as the actuality of this becoming, the Being (*ousia*), for the sake of which a thing becomes,[74] is always prior to the potentiality, the Not-Yet. Becoming towards Being means that an appearance (*eidos*) takes shape. It is the formation of a form which, as the goal of this process, is at the same time also its "beginning" (*arche*), for the process was initiated only for its sake.[75]

"Becoming follows being and is for the sake of being, but being does not follow becoming." [76] "It is not because it becomes a thing of a particular constitution that it is thus constituted, but because it is a thing of this constitution, it *becomes* a thing of this constitution." [77] The priority of *energeia* with respect to *ousia* thus implies a purposive structure, "for the sake of...," according to which the end and goal (*telos*) of a motion is at the same time its beginning (impulse or force, *arche*). The *telos* as the for-the-sake-of-which is the *energeia* of a being which determines itself according to its perfected *eidos*. Even the *dynamis* itself exists only for the sake of the *telos*; an ability exists for the actualization, not the actualization for the sake of the ability. "We do not see in order that we may have sight, but have sight that we may see." [78]

---

[72] *Ibid.*, 1049 b 24 f. ἀεὶ γὰρ ἐκ τοῦ δυνάμει ὄντος γίγνεται τὸ ἐνεργείᾳ ὄντος.
[73] Cf. *ibid.*, b 23.
[74] Cf. *De part. an.* A, 640 a 18.
[75] Cf. *Meta.* Θ 8, 1050 a 8.
[76] *De anim. gen.* E, 778 b 5 f. τῇ γὰρ οὐσίᾳ ἡ γένεσις ἀκολουθεῖ καὶ τῆς οὐσίας ἕνεκά ἐστιν, ἀλλ᾽ οὐχ αὕτη τῇ γενέσει.
[77] *Ibid.*, 778 b 2 ff. οὐ διὰ τὸ γίγνεσθαι ἕκαστον ποιόν τι, διὰ τοῦτο ποιόν τι ἐστιν,... ἀλλὰ μᾶλλον διὰ τὸ εἶναι τοιαδὶ γίγνεται τοιαῦτα.
[78] *Meta.* Θ 8, 1050 a 10 f. οὐ γὰρ ἵνα ὄψιν ἔχωσιν ὁρῶσι τὰ ζῷα ἀλλ᾽ ὅπως ὁρῶσιν ὄψιν ἔχουσιν.

Aristotle's understanding of the power of the *ousia* to determine a thing teleologically should also be briefly elucidated. This has its place not in his pursuit of the question about being as being, but in his endeavor to arrive at definitions of beings produced by art (*techne*) and of those produced by nature (*physis*), particularly of man as a unity of the soul and the body. In the interaction of the four causes [79] which bring about the generation of a being, the *techne* of making a statue, for example, which the *technites* (workman or artist) possesses is that "whence the motion begins." This is true only when the *technites* has in his soul the *eidos* of the statue he wishes to produce (the *eidos* as cause — *causa formalis*, formal cause). "For the medical art and the building art (and likewise that of statue-making and every other *techne*) are the *eidos* of health and of the house" and likewise of the statue and of every other product.[80]

The artist sees the *eidos* as that for the sake of which (*heneka tou*) the motion of the *techne* begins. It is what leads this something from its *beginning* to that *perfection* to which it is already predisposed. If the *eidos* of a statue or a house is thought of as the *telos* (*causa finalis*, final cause) in this way, then it is determinant in a genuine sense, for only as the *telos* does the *eidos* determine that and how matter (*hyle, causa materialis*, material cause) becomes active in the generation of a thing, takes on shape and embodies the thing. Thus "in one sense a house (comes) from a house," that is, "the (house) with matter from that without matter." [81] To be more precise, when the being to be produced is conceived of as *telos*, it dictates that the *technites* use a certain kind of material — gold or wood — for this particular statue to be carved and stone or tile for this particular house to be constructed.

Generally speaking, Aristotle conceives of the *technei onta*, the artificial beings, that is, those produced by men, as *ousia* taken teleologically. "For example, why is a saw such as it is? To do this and that, for this and that purpose. But this, the for-the-sake-of-which, cannot be accomplished unless the saw is made of iron; therefore it is necessary that it be made of iron, if it is to be a saw which performs its task." [82]

---

[79] With slight deviations Aristotle presented his doctrine of the four causes in several places; cf. especially these sections, to a large extent identical, in *Phys.* B 3 and *Meta.* Δ 2, as well as the beginning of *Meta.* A 3 and *An. Post.* B 11.

[80] *Meta.* Z 7, 1032 b 13 f. ἡ γὰρ ἰατρικὴ ἐστι καὶ ἡ οἰκοδομικὴ τὸ εἶδος τῆς ὑγιείας καὶ τῆς οἰκίας.

[81] *Ibid.*, b 11 ff.

[82] *Phys.* B 9, 200 a 10 ff.

Aristotle likewise conceived of the realm of the *physei onta*, of beings by nature, in such a way that their substantiality is one of the causes in the sense of the for-the-sake-of-which.

"If a house, for example, had been a thing made by nature, it would have been made in the same way as it is now by art; and if things made by nature were made also by art, they would come to be in the same way as nature."[83] All natural production occurs "for the sake of an end (*telos*)" [84] and not out of mere necessity. For this reason Aristotle emphatically contests the assertion "that, for example, the teeth grow in out of (mere) necessity (*ex anankes*), the front teeth sharp, fitted for cutting, the molars broad and useful for grinding down food."[85] Instead he emphasizes the teleological character of the specific constitution of the organs. Although in nature there is no "rational action" as we know it in human *techne*, "it is clear that when it is both by nature and for an end that the swallow makes its nest and the spider its web, and plants grow leaves for the sake of the fruit and send their roots down, not up, for the sake of nourishment, this kind of cause does exist in beings which come to be by nature." [86]

The various stages in the physical process of formation do not stand next to one another, indifferently. They are structured in such a way that each one serves the other in reaching a common *telos*, "if nothing interferes." [87] Aristotle recognized that failures (*hamartemata*) [88] and obstacles are possible within teleological relationships in *physis*. In spite of this, natural things always or "for the most part" [89] arrive at their predetermined perfection. "In everything which has a definite *telos* what precedes and what follows occurs for the sake of the *telos*." [90] For Aristotle this holds true in a particular way for the soul. In *De Anima* we read: "It is clear that the soul is also the for-the-sake-of-which cause (of the body), for *physis*, like *nous*, always does whatever it does for the sake of something, and this something is its end. In the case of animals (and also of plants) this end is naturally the soul." [91]

---

[83] *Ibid.*, B 8, 199 a 12-15.
[84] *Ibid.*, a 31 f. τοῦ τέλους δὲ ἕνεκα.
[85] *Ibid.*, 198 b 24 ff.
[86] *Ibid.*, 199 a 26 ff.
[87] *Ibid.*, 199 a 10 f.; cf. 199 b 26.
[88] *Ibid.*, 199 b 4.
[89] *Ibid.*, 199 b 24 ὡς ἐπὶ τὸ πολύ.
[90] *Ibid.*, 199 a 8 f. ἐν ὅσοις τέλος ἔστι τι, τούτου ἕνεκα πράττεται τὸ πρότερον καὶ τὸ ἐφεξῆς. Hardie and Gaye (Ross ed.) translate : "...where a series has a completion, all the preceding steps are for the sake of that."
[91] *De An.* B 1, 415 b 15 ff. φανερὸν δ' ὡς καὶ οὗ ἕνεκεν ἡ ψυχὴ αἰτία, ὥσπερ γὰρ ὁ νοῦς

The very teleological character of the *physei on* which is the *synholon* (whole) of body and soul and especially the character of man shows how *dynamis* and *energeia*, potentiality and actuality, ground together or furnish the cause of this essential being in its unity. It also shows how *energeia* is the dominant one of these two. As *telos*, *energeia* not only effects the unity of man's body and soul, but also guides his powers toward their perfection. This may be elucidated with the aid of some passages from *De Anima*.

In the first chapter of the second book of *De Anima* Aristotle seeks a general determination of the soul and arrives at this result: "Thus the soul is the first grade of actuality of a natural body which potentially has life." [92] The natural body is the *hyle* related to the *eidos*, soul, in such a way that, in the former, actuality finds its own potentiality. Because the *eidos* is the *telos* or — as Aristotle writes here — the "*entelecheia*" [93] of the potential *hyle*, of a natural body, it determines the body. As a *telos*, the soul constitutes this unity in thus "producing this living thing"; it takes the body in its hand, so to speak, as it would a tool and thus actualizes it as an organized and ordered unity. "All natural bodies

---

ἕνεκά του ποιεῖ, τὸν αὐτὸν τρόπον καὶ ἡ φύσις, καὶ τοῦτ᾽ ἔστι αὐτῆς τέλος· τοιοῦτον δ᾽ἐν τοῖς ζῴοις ἡ ψυχὴ κατὰ φύσιν.

[92] *De An.* B 1, 412 a 27 f. διὸ ἡ ψυχή ἐστιν ἐντελέχεια ἡ πρώτη σώματος φυσικοῦ δυνάμει ζωὴν ἔχοντος. J. A. Smith (Ross ed.) translates : "That is why the soul is the first grade of actuality of a natural body having life potentially in it."

[93] How the meanings of *energeia* and *entelecheia* are to be differentiated from one another is an old problem in the interpretation of Aristotle. The difficulty is that in Aristotle's usage of the terms a consistent distinction between the two cannot be established. Often it seems that they can even be exchanged with one another (cf. Düring, p. 617, n. 195; Stallmach, p. 188). Furthermore the two passages (1047 a 30; 1050 a 22. Ross translates *energeia* with "actuality," *entelecheia* with "complete reality.") in which Aristotle connects the two terms allude to their being synonymous. Nonetheless, the fact that in the case of *entelecheia* Aristotle invented a new word may refer to his intention to emphasize a certain nuance or aspect of the concept of actuality, even if he did not carry out this intention in his later use of the terms. If, for Aristotle, "actuality" signifies the process of actualization as well as the state of being actualized (the *telos*) itself, then if one makes the distinction between a way and the destination to which it leads, one can see how *entelecheia* could assume the aspect of perfection (of the *telos*), whereas *energeia* would stand for aspect of becoming. Here it must be emphasized that this would be an attempt at a genetic explanation which does not take into consideration that the term *energeia* itself can always just as well indicate the aspect of perfection. Thus, taken linguistically, it fluctuates between a *nomen actionis* and a *nomen acti*. In this attempt at an explanation we are obligated to the well-balanced presentation in Stallmach, *op. cit.*, p. 182 ff.

are tools of the soul," [94] and they exist "for the sake of the soul," [95] which is the goal to be reached. Taken in this way, the soul is not a part of a thing absolutely separate from the body; nor is it a quality or quantity of the body. Instead, it is that *energeia* which determines and unifies the *hyle* of the *dynamis* of the living thing; as the *telos*, it is the "fulfilment" of the *dynamis*.

Insofar as Aristotle defines the soul as *energeia* or *entelecheia*, he can also call it "life." [96] With respect to life's various functions he distinguishes between different "parts of the soul," its powers or possibilities, beginning with the nutritive, self-propagating soul, proceeding to the perceiving soul, then the appetitive, up to the function of the soul which occurs in man alone, namely, *noesis*, intuitive understanding. For Aristotle, this last function represents the fulfilment of all the possibilities of the soul and thus the *energeia*, conceived as the *telos*, of the soul as a whole.

As we already showed in Part One of this book, *noesis* occurs as a spontaneous, energetic principle, as *"nous poietikos"* (see above, p. 6). But although this spontaneously active power of thinking fulfils the meaning of *energeia* as *telos* in the purest manner, it still remains bound to its correlate, the *dynamis*, to potentiality and materiality. As we saw, the *nous poietikos* is still dependent upon the *nous pathetikos*.[97]

---

[94] *De An.* B 4, 415 b 18 f. πάντα γὰρ τὰ φυσικὰ σώματα τῆς ψυχῆς ὄργανα. J. A. Smith (Ross ed.) translates: "All natural bodies are organs of the soul."
[95] *Ibid.*, b 20 ...ἕνεκα τῆς ψυχῆς Smith translates: "...that for the sake of which they are is soul."
[96] Cf. *ibid.*, B 2, 413 a 20 - b 10.
[97] Cf. *ibid.*, Γ 5, 430 a 10 ff.

PART THREE

ONTOLOGY (OUSIOLOGY) AND THEOLOGY

However, does the thought that *energeia* is ontologically prior to *dynamis* not imply that ultimately there must be an *energeia* not preceded by *dynamis*? In relation to what is "prior with regard to *ousia*" [1] — which encompasses the other two kinds of priority as well (see above, p. 38) — Aristotle showed in the eighth chapter of book Theta [2] that in a decisive sense [3] there must be something absolutely intransient, eternal (*aidion*), free of all potentiality, of all inability-to-be, always actual, which exists of necessity (*ex anankes on*)[4] and as such is something primary (*proton*).[5] In these terms Aristotle conceives of the "eternal things" which are perpetually in a state of actualization and cannot convert into their opposite. In this context he shows explicitly why there must be things of pure *energeia*, intransient and eternal primary things (*prota*): "If these did not exist, nothing at all would exist." [6] Aristotle expressly made this original *energeia* an object of his reflections; the philosophy which addresses itself to it is theology.

In Book Lambda Aristotle already discussed the irresolvable aporia which would arise if one wanted to think of the *principle* of motion (*kinesis*) also in terms of *dynamis*. In this discussion, he showed that a certain primary being has to be assumed. Since there are moved things, there must be movers. The final mover, however, cannot be a moved-mover which moves by virtue of another mover, for then it would only

---

[1] *Meta.* Θ 8, 1050 b 6 ff.

[2] Cf. on the following Joseph Stallmach: *Dynamis und Energeia*, Meisenheim/Glan, 1959, p. 135.

[3] Cf. κυριωτέρως, *ibid.*, b 6. Ross translates: "in a strict sense."

[4] Cf. *ibid.*, b 18.

[5] Cf. *ibid.*, b 19.

[6] εἰ γὰρ ταῦτα μὴ ἦν, οὐθὲν ἂν ἦν. *Ibid.*, b 19. Ross translates: "For if these did not exist, nothing would exist."

be a mediator (*meson*).[7] Instead, it must be an "unmoved-mover" (*akineton kinoun*), a being which is eternal, is a substance (*ousia*) existing by itself. Above all, it is *energeia*, pure actuality and activeness, [8] which does not have to be actualized within the genetic series of *dynamis* and *energeia*.

For Aristotle, *energeia* is "better" [9] than *dynamis* because the *dynamei on*, still in need of fulfilment, is as nothing. But the thought that *energeia* is ontologically prior to *dynamis* also implies that the priority requires something primary as pure *energeia*. Because of its self-sufficiency [10] as pure *energeia*, this primate is the perfect, the good and the best.[11] As such, this "best" [12] is the ultimate for-the-sake-of-which, the ultimate ground (*arche*), the ultimate end (*telos*) of everything which is moved. Aristotle conceived of this motion on the model of continual motion in space (*phora*), linking the end (*telos*) with the beginning (*arche*) in just the way that the first heaven, according to Aristotle, moves in a circle.[13] That primary, best, and necessary being which, as *telos*, is the cause of perfect motion in space and — by means of further, complex principles of motion — of the motion of the whole universe of beings is God, *theos*. "Thus it is a being which exists of necessity and it is good, insofar as it is necessary, and in this sense, it is *arche*.... On such a principle depend heaven and nature." [14]

In this sense the definition of pure *energeia* conceived as God is teleological. Because of final causality, the sensible universe depends upon a non-sensible God, existing separately and unmoved. The perfect essence moves in such a way that it arouses love and desire in all other beings. "It (the *proton kinoun*) moves as a beloved moves and through what is moved by it, it moves other things."[15] Ultimately, however, for Aristotle the uniqueness of God as a beloved can lie only

---

[7] *Meta. Λ* 7, 1072 a 24.
[8] *Ibid.*, a 25 f.
[9] Θ 9, 1051 a 15 βελτίων.
[10] *Cf.* N 4, 1091 b 16 f.
[11] Cf. A 2, 982 b 6 f.
[12] Cf. *Λ* 7, 1072 a 35 f. ἄριστον.
[13] *Ibid.*, a 21 ff.
[14] *Ibid.*, b 10-14 ἐξ ἀνάγκης ἄρα ἐστὶν ὄν· καὶ ᾗ ἀνάγκη, καλῶς, καὶ οὕτως ἀρχή ... ἐκ τοιαύτης ἄρα ἀρχῆς ἤρτηται ὁ οὐρανὸς καὶ ἡ φύσις. Ross translates: "The first mover, then, exists of necessity, its mode of being is good, and it is in this sense a first principle...On such a principle, then, depend the heavens and the world of nature."
[15] *Ibid.*, b 3 f. κινεῖ δὲ ὡς ἐρώμενον, κινουμένῳ δὲ τἆλλα κινεῖ. Ross translates: "The final cause, then, produces motion as being loved, but all other things move by being moved."

in that principle which he considers the highest of all, the principle of *nous*. The moving force of God moves in the same way as "what is desired and what is rationally apprehended." [16] The uniqueness of God lies ultimately in the complete actuality of his thinking (see above, p. 10) which — ever "awake" [17] — has the absolutely best[18] as its object.

But what exactly is this "best" which God, in his eternal blessedness (*eudaimonia*) has as his object when he thinks of thinking — *noesis noeseos* (see above, p. 7, n. 23)? Does this signify a pure relation of thought to itself, where the object is free of all determination? Is Aristotle a precursor of modern philosophy of reflection, although he could not fully develop this aspect of self-reflection? [19] Or does the Aristotelian God have other "gods" within his divine thinking? Does the *nous-theos* have as his object the other *noes* which belong to it, the other movers of the celestial spheres? Recently it has been very persuasively argued [20] that a "specific determinate content" has to be found for divine thought and that the Aristotelian concept of God has to be taken as inherently pluralistic. Then the *noesis noeseos* is not reflection, conceived in the modern sense as a relation of the *cogitatum* (thought) back to the *ego cogito* (I think); instead, it is "purely objective" being-by-itself. By way of its objects, the *noes*, the divine *nous* is able to think of itself: it becomes *noetos*. The self-relatedness of thinking [21] is mediated by its objects [22] with which it is in a certain sense identical. Even if one assumes that divine thought is in this way expressly mediated by its "objects,"

---

[16] 1072 a 26. τὸ ὀρεκτὸν καὶ τὸ νοητόν. Ross translates: "The object of desire and the object of thought."

[17] Cf. Λ 9, 1074 b 17 f.

[18] Λ 7, 1072 b 18-30.

[19] This is the view in K. Oehler: *Die Lehre vom noetischen und dianoetischen Denken bei Platon und Aristoteles, op. cit.*, p. 205 ff. In reply to the works by H. J. Krämer mentioned in n. 20, Oehler writes: "Instead, we can ascertain that Aristotle did not effect a realization of the concept of God's thinking-of-himself." On this point, cf. the metacritique by H. J. Krämer: "Grundfragen der aristotelischen Theologie" (in the following notes abbreviated as "Grundfragen") in: *Theologie und Philosophie*, Vol. 44, No. 3, 1969, n. 55.

[20] We are referring here to H. J. Krämer, first in *Der Ursprung der Geistesmetaphysik*, Amsterdam 1964², 1967, 127-199 (abbreviated in the following: UGM); then in "Zur geschichtlichen Stellung der aristotelischen Metaphysik" (abbreviated in the following: GSAM), *Kantstudien* 58, 1967, p. 313 ff., for the last time in "Grundfragen."

[21] Λ 7, 1072 b 19 f.

[22] *Ibid.*, b 20 f.

the *noes*, it remains the case that the pure actuality and activeness of God lies in his being with himself as the purely rational.[23]

With this we conclude our discussion of the more exact definition of God's being-separated and being-unmoved and the determination of his relationship to the *noes*, the subject of what has been called Aristotle's

---

[23] With reference to *Λ* 7 and 9 where, according to Krämer, Aristotle understands the divine *nous* and his self-relatedness (*Selbstbezüglichkeit*) in analogy to human thinking, the "specific, determinate content" would have to meet two requirements. On the one hand, as a content it must be distinct from divine thinking (as a process) itself; on the other hand, it could not be something outside of divine thought, since then, as an external cause or occasion for thought it would contradict the perfect actuality of God. Hence, the entire realm of all materiality cannot possibly become an object of thinking here (cf. "Grundfragen", p. 372 ff., *GSAM*, p. 316 and n. 10, with the interesting reference to *Pol.* H 3, 1325 b 28 ff., also *Meta. Λ* 9, 1075 a 5 ff., especially a 7). The second requirement is that this content must be sought in the divine itself, and thus in the realm of the "primary *ousia*." The first leads to the assumption that the *prote ousia* is internally differentiated, since one could not otherwise conceive of a distinct content of divine thinking. The "primary *ousia*" has to be taken as pluralistic in order that "one part" of the divine be able to relate to "another part" (cf. *UGM* II, p. 127 ff.; *GSAM*, p. 318 and n. 17, 18; "Grundfragen," p. 368-370). Indeed, there is in Aristotle such a pluralization of the concept of God. In the context of his cosmological reflections he posits fifty-five *theoi* next to the one and primary *theos*, conceived of as the "unmoved mover" of the whole universe (1074 b 2). There is good reason for seeing the object suited to the supreme *nous* in these fifty-five "gods," fixed as movers of the celestical spheres. In the first place, as something divine they meet the requirement that they may not be anything outside of divine thinking itself, but in the second place, they are not absolutely identical with it. As *nous-theos* the Aristotelian God thinks the *noes* which belong to him — in whatever way. God's thinking, which thus thinks aspects of itself, is a "purely objective being-with-itself, in which thinking loses itself in complete surrender to its object. It merges with its object, becomes one with it and consequently, insofar as it thinks this object, it thinks itself along with it." (*GSAM*, p. 319). According to Krämer the relationship of these movers of the spheres (= planets) to the mover of the heavens (= mover of the world) should be conceived as one of "immanence" (*GSAM*, p. 318 f.; "Grundfragen," p. 375 ff.; *UGM*, p. 167 ff.) in connection with which the mover of the world must be conceived of as the "all-embracing, unifying concept" ("*Inbegriff*") of the whole uppermost realm of being of which other essences (*Wesenheiten*) are only aspects. As immaterial essences the *theoi* or *noes* are supreme reality and thus to be thought of as God. Krämer finds indications of this (*GSAM*, p. 319, n. 20) in *De caelo* 279 a 21 f.; cf. on this point *UGM*, p. 169 f., where Krämer draws this conclusion from the actual identity of thinking and the object of thought in divine thinking. Krämer's thesis that the divine *nous* is related to the *noes* (movers of celestial spheres) as an "objective thinking-substrate" ("*objektives Denksubstrat*") becomes more persuasive when, as Krämer did, one regards Aristotelian theology in the context of Xenocrates and the Academic metaphysics of the elements. Even though the mathematical structure peculiar to the philosophy of the Academy appears to be largely dismantled in Aristotle (cf. however *Λ* 8, 1073 a 14-23, b 1-8, reminiscent of the "idea-numbers" of the Academicians) nevertheless the similarity to this Xenocratic-Academic model is noteworthy. We find a unified principle which is nevertheless pluralistically structured (*UGM*, p. 171).

"theology." What does the existence of such a theology mean for our question concerning the philosophical theory of being as being which we have discussed in this treatise beginning with Book Gamma? Is there a connection between the theology in Book Lambda and the philosophical theory developed in Books Zeta, Eta, and Theta? From the first commentators on Aristotle, Theophrastus and Alexander of Aphrodisias, until the twelfth century [24] it was regarded as certain that there was only *one* First Science, theology. Then in the late scholastic philosophy the view began to take hold that, on the one hand, Aristotelian metaphysics was a universal science of Being, investigating being as such — the *ens commune* — and, on the other hand, that it was a science whose only object was the unmoved and separated being, that is, the science of theology. Both concepts of metaphysics (*metaphysica generalis* and *metaphysica specialis* as *theologia*) claim a place in the *Corpus Aristotelicum*.

At the end of the last century the discussion was reopened on the question of whether for Aristotle there is only *one* primary philosophical science, theology *or* "ontology," or whether they both exist side by side and how in the latter case this relationship be determined. One problem in particular presents difficulties, namely, how the statements about this science in the seventh chapter of Book Kappa as well as in the first chapter of Book Epsilon relate to those in Book Gamma which we have discussed. In Epsilon[25] we read: "But if there is something which is eternal and immovable and separated, clearly the knowledge of it belongs to a theoretical science — not, however, to physics (for physics deals with certain movable things) nor to mathematics, but to a science prior to both. For physics deals with things which exist separately but are not immovable, and some parts of mathematics deal with things which are immovable but presumably do not exist separately, but as embodied in *hyle*; but the 'first' science deals with things which exist separately and are immovable. Now all causes must be eternal, but especially these; for they are the cause of whatever of the eternal things appears to us. There must, then, be three theoretical philosophies: mathematics, physics, and theology, since it is obvious that if the divine is present anywhere, it is present in things of this sort; and the highest science must deal with the highest objects."

---

[24] Cf. on this point: Owens, *The Doctrine of Being in the Aristotelian Metaphysics*, Toronto, 1951, p. 4-11.
[25] 1026 a 10 ff. We have adopted Ross' translation, with some slight changes.

Later Aristotle notes the following: "Now one can raise the question whether first philosophy (*prote philosophia*) is universal (*katholou*) or deals with one genus and one single entity." [26] He answers this question himself in the following way: "If there were no being other than those beings which are formed by nature, then physics (Ross translates "natural science" — *Tr.*) would be the first science (*prote episteme*); but if there is an immovable being (*ousia akinetos*), the science of this must be prior and must be first philosophy, and universal, because it is the first. And it will belong to this to contemplate being as being — both what it is and the attributes which belong to it."

These passages do not leave any doubt that Aristotle has only *one* science in view here, a science which deals with being and considers this being immovable and separate. This first science is theology. In Book Kappa the text is just as unequivocal. In several passages Aristotle characterizes the science of being as being, which treats universally of what is immovable and exists separately, as theology. For example, in 1064 b ff. it is stated: "Evidently, there are three kinds of theoretical sciences — physics, mathematics, and theology. The highest class of the sciences is the theoretical and of these themselves the last named is the highest, because it has to do with the highest being." Following this we read: "One might raise the question whether the science of being as being should be regarded as universal or not." [27] This question is answered as follows: "...but if there is another entity and substance, which exists separately and is immovable, then the science which deals with it must be different from and prior to physics, and universal because it is prior." [28]

The question is, however, how these statements relate to those in Book Gamma and to what extent the program outlined there — and carried out in Books Zeta, Eta, and Theta — agrees with them. More precisely, questions of the following sort arise: Does the characterization of the metaphysical question in Book Gamma as the question of *on hei on* mean the same thing as it does in Books Epsilon and Kappa?

---

[26] 1026 a 23 ff. ἀπορήσειε γὰρ ἄν τις, πότερόν ποθ' ἡ πρώτη φιλοσοφία καθόλου ἐστὶν ἢ περί τι γένος καὶ φύσιν τινὰ μίαν. We have adopted Ross' version, with some slight changes.

[27] 1064 b 6 ff.

[28] 1064 b 11 ff. εἰ δὲ ἔστιν ἑτέρα φύσις καὶ οὐσία χωριστὴ καὶ ἀκίνητος, ἑτέραν ἀνάγκη καὶ τὴν ἐπιστήμην αὐτῆς εἶναι καὶ προτέραν τῆς φυσικῆς καὶ καθόλου τῷ προτέραν. Translations adopted from Ross, with slight changes.

Is *ousia* itself conceived in both books as the "first" (*prote*), even if not *verbatim*? Is the meaning of the "being-separate" and "being-immovable" of *ousia* in Epsilon and Kappa the same as that in Book Gamma? Do certain passages at the end of this book [29] indicate such a meaning? Is it for this very reason that the philosophical theory in Gamma is "first" philosophy and as such is therefore theology? Or is it theology for a different reason? Furthermore, one has to inquire into (see also above, p. X) the special sense of "universal" in Gamma 1003 a 24 (as well as in 1005 a 35) and investigate what "universal" means in Epsilon and Kappa and how its meaning there can be made compatible with its meaning in Gamma.

These and many other questions have been raised in recent exegetical attempts to determine the character of Aristotelian metaphysics. Aside from these there are also investigations in current scholarship on Aristotle dealing with this question from the standpoint of the history of the development of Aristotle's philosophy. Furthermore, there are also investigations attempting to answer the question about the character of philosophical theory by reflecting upon the issue underlying Aristotle's fundamental concepts.

The discussion was opened by Paul Natorp,[30] who came to the conclusion that Aristotelian metaphysics cannot be equated with a "theology." According to Natorp, the question of being as being concerns "the most universal, the most abstract of all that can be the object of scientific investigation." It is an "insufferable contradiction" to assume that that first philosophy, which deals in this way with being in general and as such, could be identical with a science which deals with a special realm of being, as theology does. It is impossible "that on the one hand *prote philosophia* is supposed to be the universal *philosophia*, laying a foundation for all others, but on the other hand should be one and the same as that science concerned with immaterial, unchanging Being as the most eminent genus of being." [31] Natorp suggested that those passages which would contradict his view that Aristotle's philosophical theory is an "ontology" be deleted as later interpolations by the early Peripatetics.[32]

---

[29] 1009 a 36-38; 1010 a 25-35; 1012 b 29-31.
[30] Paul Natorp : "Thema und Disposition der Aristotelischen Metaphysik." In: *Philosophische Monatshefte*, XXIV, 1888.
[31] *Ibid.*, p. 49-50, cf. also p. 52-53.
[32] *Ibid.*, p. 51-52; 55.

By means of an investigation of the history of the development of
Aristotle's philosophy, Werner Jaeger [33] also came to the conclusion
that two contradictory views can be found in Aristotle's definition of
philosophical theory, a contradiction which Aristotle noticed himself.
At the beginning of Gamma 1, first philosophy was clearly characterized
as a "universal science" and opposed to special sciences and individual
realms of being. In Epsilon 1 and Kappa 7 the "highest species of
being" was called the object of the first science. On the other hand,
Aristotle could not and did not claim that the immaterial movers of
the heavens were not "special beings" of some "special kind of being."
According to Jaeger, these two views of metaphysics "could not have been
produced by one and the same creative act." Instead, here two fundamentally different trains of thought have been meshed with one another,
and it is readily apparent that the theological and Platonic one is the
older of the two. If metaphysics was later defined as the theory of being
as being, then this definition was based on the view that reality is a
"great, unified, graduated structure." This would be the "more Aristotelian" view, that is, the view corresponding to the characteristic phase
in Aristotle's development. Thus, for Jaeger, first philosophy is the science
of being as being, a universal science of being as such.

In the first phase in the development of this thinking Martin
Heidegger [34] had already pointed out the "dual characteristic" of *prote
philosophia*. According to him, *prote philosophia* consists of knowledge
of being as being as well as knowledge of the highest realm of being
(*timiotaton genos*) out of which the totality of beings is determined.[35]

This problem of the "difference" and "correlation" has engaged
Heidegger ever anew.[36] In a lecture given in 1957 [37] he tried to articulate
step by step the movement which underlies both. He did so in an effort to
show why metaphysics historically came to be an "ontology," for which
Being is the "ground" (cause) of every entity, and at the same time a
"theology," for which the highest being (God) "grounds" everything.

In all of the publications on this problem appearing in the last twenty
years, the distinction can again be made between exegetical investigations,

---

[33] *Aristoteles*, Berlin, 1923, pp. 226-228. (Eng. tr., 2nd Ed., 1948, p. 217 ff.)
[34] Cf. on the following by the author: *Heidegger and the Tradition*, Evanston, 1972.
[35] First in: *Was ist Metaphysik?* Frankfurt, 1929, p. 19. (Eng. tr. *What is Metaphysics?* tr. R. F. C. Hull, A. Crick, in : *Existence and Being*, ed. W. Brock, Chicago
1949; cf. *Kant und das Problem der Metaphysik*. Frankfurt/Main², 1950, p. 17. (Eng.
tr. *Kant and the Problem of Metaphysics*, tr. James Churchill, Bloomington, Indiana,
1962.)

development-historical investigations, and investigations from the standpoint of the history of ideas. We will not pursue the development-historical attempts any further here.[38] We will, however, take some examples from exegetical and idea-historical investigations. In this way we will show that these too still waver between the three possibilities: that metaphysics is simply theology, that it is simply ontology, or that it is both ontology (ousiology) and theology.

By means of a detailed exegetical discussion of questions of the sort mentioned above, Ph. Merlan [39] arrived at the first conclusion, that philosophical theory is only theology. On the basis of a thorough interpretation of Epsilon 1 and Kappa 3-7 he presents the view that the object of the theory in Gamma 1, the *on hei on*, is not an "abstract universal." Here as elsewhere it is the first substance (*prote ousia*) the realm of being "separately existent," "immovable," subsistent, and intelligible. According to Merlan, to reach a fundamental conception of what the concept "universal" means in Book Gamma, one must consider that Aristotle's purpose here was to inquire into principles. This inquiry followed the procedure of the Platonic Academy; the structures of fundamental opposite poles — One-Many, Identity-Difference, Being-Non-Being — were investigated, and since they constitute the highest sphere of Being, they were treated as the cause of each of the lower spheres derived from it. As an investigation within the tradition of the Platonic Academy, the purpose of the investigation of being "in general" (universally, *katholou*) as Being was to show that, in every being based on principles, the highest sphere of being is present. This is the sphere of the principle of the first substance (*prote ousia*), of the first "being" (*proton on*), of the first One (*proton hen*), of the "self-same" itself (*tauton auto*) as a "universal cause." In a way very similar to that practiced in the Platonic Academy, the Aristotelian philosopher asks with regard to these principles: What lends being existence, unity, and identity? Particularly in 1026 a 30-31 Merlan finds support for the view that as the highest sphere of Being, as a universal ("as a *katholou*," p. 146), the *prote ousia* is thought to be present in every being. Kappa 3-7 as

---

[36] Cf. on this point especially: Heidegger: *Nietzsche*, Vol. II, Pfullingen 1961, p. 348 ff.

[37] "Die Onto-theologische Verfassung der Metaphysik", Pfullingen 1957, p. 31.

[38] Cf. on this point the review by H. Wagner, in : *Philosophische Rundschau*, 1959, No. 2, p. 129 ff.

[39] *From Platonism to Neoplatonism*, The Hague, 1953, p. 132 ff.

well supports his positions. In that section the method is conceived
as a "transition" (*aphairesis*) from the universal-concrete within itself
to a state of being present (p. 147 ff.). In any case, for Merlan the science
of being as being in Gamma is just as much "first philosophy" in the
sense of a theology as it is in Epsilon and Kappa.[40]

By means of a "reconstruction" (p. 289) of Aristotelian metaphysics,
J. Owens [41] came to the conclusion that philosophical science as the
science of being as being proceeds by means of *pros hen*-determinations
(see above, p. 16), of the highest nature of *ousia* derivatively present
in all individually sensible beings. This nature proves to be form which,
as *energeia*, constitutes the cause of an individual being. For Owens, the
ousia defined in this way — insofar as it is the "primary instance" [42] —
is identical with the divine, separately existent, first *ousia*. This position
involves certain difficulties. For example, in Book Lambda the divine
ousia is not defined according to the *pros hen*-method. Furthermore,
it must be conceded that Aristotle did not carry out the program defined
in Books Alpha and Epsilon. Nevertheless, according to Owens, the
separately existent, first *ousia* represents the object of the highest philosophy. This first *ousia* must be sought through sensible being. The
meaning of Being which governed the conception of the Being of being
from Parmenides to Plato is still that of the Aristotelian supra-sensibly
existent divine which sensible beings "imitate."[43]

Some years later, by means of yet a different construction of Aristotelian metaphysics, G. Patzig [44] arrived at the conclusion that, in any
case, during a particular phase in Aristotle's thinking, metaphysics as
the science of Being was theology. Patzig begins with the so-called
"paronymic" (*pros hen*) structure of Aristotelian science as a science of
Being. According to this structure the wholeness of this science is determined by the relationship of the individual modes of Being (categories)
to the eminent mode of being (*ousia*). For Aristotle, this part of the

---

[40] "Postscript zu einer Besprechung" in: *Philosophische Rundschau*, VII, 1959,
p. 148 ff.
We are indebted to H. J. Krämer for having deepened our insight into the influence
of the Platonic-academic doctrine upon Aristotle, *GSAM*, p. 313 ff.; in particular,
the chapter "Zur aristotelischen Ontologie," p. 337 ff., investigates very precisely the
various series of derivations and the *pros hen*-structure; cf. *II. Teil, Anm.* 3.
[41] *Op. cit.*
[42] P. 291.
[43] P. 229; cf. Preface to 2nd Ed., p. 23.
[44] G. Patzig : "Theologie und Ontologie in der 'Metaphysik' des Aristoteles."
Kantstudien 52, 1960/61, p. 185 ff.

paronymic structure is the "proton" (the First, Primary). Everything else enters into a relationship of "dependency" upon it. Hence, the paronymic science of Being has to deal "principally" with the "first being," *ousia*, because it is a mediator, the science of *ousia* becomes the science of all other being, of the other categories, as well. This holds true first of all for the realm of "natural" substance. To this extent this view has a solid foundation in the text. Patzig's thesis with regard to the connection between ontology and theology consists, however, to a certain extent, in a repetition of the paronymic structure in the relationship of natural substance to divine substance. According to Patzig, the ontology of natural substance would remain incomplete if it were not again paronymically grounded in a relationship to the "proton." Just as the natural *ousia* as a kind of category is the *proton* for all other beings, the divine *ousia* is the *proton* for natural *ousiai*. Therefore, for Patzig, theology is the doctrine of the "first substance" among the other substances, the "genuine substance" from which all other substances "borrow" their being. For Patzig, it follows from this that the science of being as such is theology.[45]

Rather than offering an exegesis or a reconstruction of Aristotle's philosophy, H. Boeder [46] has reflected upon Aristotle's fundamental concepts from the point of view of the history of ideas. More precisely, by recalling "the history of first philosophy, the crisis in its principles" (p. 112) which can be seen in the development of its fundamental principles from Parmenides to Plato and the Sophists, he challenged most decisively the view that it is possible to understand Aristotle's ontology

---

[45] Nonetheless, in the later books of the Metaphysics Patzig sees the dissolution of "the coherence of a double paronymic ontology." Here the reduction of the *ousiai* to a divine *proton* can no longer be detected. According to Patzig this represents the process of a "de-paronymization of the philosophical doctrine of principles" which can also be observed elsewhere in Aristotle. The place of paronymy as a methodological principle is taken over by analogy. A relationship is no longer defined as a relationship of different things to something identical (such as the "first," as with paronymy), but as an identical relationship to different things (proportional analogy). Thus, according to Patzig, Aristotle's development does not progress, as Jaeger claimed, from a "theologizing" to an "ontologizing" phase. Within ontology itself it progresses from the paronymical to the analogical method. According to Patzig, this development does away with the correlation of ontology and theology. This would explain why theology, which occupied the center of the inquiries of Book Lambda, is not mentioned any more in Books Zeta, Eta, and Theta. (For a critique on this point: W. Bröcker: *Aristoteles*. Frankfurt, 1964, p. 236 ff.; and more recently: H. J. Krämer: *GSAM*, p. 342).

[46] H. Boeder: Weshalb "Sein des Seienden?" In: *Philosophisches Jahrbuch*, 78, 1971, p. 111 f.

as a universal science of Being. According to Boeder, the theory of being as being is "first philosophy," and first philosophy is theology, because it has to do exclusively with the first (primary) as origin and cause of beings. Only because of this primary something, this origin and cause, is first philosophy "universal" in the sense that it treats of "of being as such with a view to the whole" (p. 113). This first something is that particular being whose primacy, according to Boeder, lies in its being-separated and its being-not-in-movement. This he sees in the origin of these terms as a development in the history of philosophy. To be more precise, Boeder regards the theory of being as being as the "first" theory "because it directs and attaches itself to what exists separately and without any kind of transitions" (p. 114). Boeder thus seems to assume that the object of first philosophy is consistently raised from one level to the next. Philosophy begins with the contemplation of what is perceptible by sense, what is "more readily familiar" because of its immediacy (p. 122). Its object is the "simple" as the "what," the essence which it has to mark as a kind of primary substance ("*Art von Erstem*") (p. 120). This is followed by theoretical contemplation of the *axiomata* always presupposed by all knowledge, and among these, the axiomatic foundation to which all other axioms are related, as expressed in the law of contradiction.[47] According to Boeder, the next level in the gradations of the objects of philosophical theory is the rational insight which touches the "simple" as the "true." In this rational, immediate being-in-the-presence of that which is simple and actual lies for Boeder the presence of a being itself, the actuality of a being. The object of philosophical theory does not reach its full concretion, however, until it exhibits the "this." The "this" emerges in the purely rational apprehension of the apprehensible as the "purely rational." Its "entire actuality is the activity of the apprehension of the simple" being "the first entity and the cause of all other entities" (p. 122). The "this," however, is not a Platonic idea; it is God. He fulfils purely and fully the two aspects of separateness and absence of transition. All the preceding objects of theory are ordered towards him.

According to I. Düring,[48] the Aristotelian first philosophy treats of being "universally" and for him that means "in a universal-abstract sense" (p. 599). Unlike Merlan, Düring understands the passage in

---

[47] Cf. H. Boeder: "Das Prinzip des Widerspruchs oder der Sachverhalt als Sachverhalt." In: *Festschrift für Eugen Fink*, The Hague, 1965.
[48] *Op. cit.*, p. 591 f.

Epsilon cited earlier (see above, p. 48) [49] to mean that first philosophy is not a "philosophy of the universal" but a "universal philosophy." [50] The definition of first philosophy in Epsilon as *theologike* does not mean that its object is the separately existing and immovable *prote ousia*, especially since the term *prote ousia* does not occur there at all. Instead, as first philosophy it is a "philosophy of the first things." Only "for the sake of a tidy system" did it occur to Aristotle to call this First Science theology (p. 117). To be sure, Düring does not deny that the early Aristotle, particularly in Book Lambda, may have had a theological conception of the object of philosophy. At that time philosophy was in fact the science of "what exists without a share in natural process" (p. 116). But for Düring only the later conception of the object of philosophy is decisive. Düring adds this remark to his observations: "It seems to me that the time has come to give up the expression 'Aristotle's theology' or to assign it to its rightful, unassuming place. It was a mere whim that Aristotle sought a term in order to reach the nice number of three" (p. 117).[51]

By means of an exegetical investigation, A. Mansion [52] presented the view that Aristotelian philosophy is neither simply an ontology nor simply a theology, but both. He insists upon distinguishing between a science which inquires into being as being — which he designates as "metaphysics" or "*philosophie suprême*" — and a theory which proceeds as theology and "first philosophy" (*philosophie première*), the topic of which is the "individual being." In 1005 a 33 - b 1 Mansion finds full support for the view that the former treats of being abstract-universally. In Epsilon 1 he finds the definition of "First Philosophy," but at the same time he readily concedes that the term "universal" in 1026 a 27-32 could also be interpreted in the sense of the abstract-universal, and not in the sense of the concrete-individual, as he interpreted it. He does not regard the difficulty which arises in Kappa as decisive because, with additional support from the text, he opts for the familiar view that the contents of this book cannot have been genuine statements by Aristotle.[53]

---

[49] 1026 a 29-31.

[50] Düring, *op. cit.*, p. 599.

[51] Not long ago W. Bröcker, *op. cit.*, p. 232 f., advocated the view that Aristotle meant by the expression *katholou* not the general, but the "total" which "as such comprises in itself everything general as well as special." According to Bröcker, ontology is theology in the sense that both are a "science of the whole of being."

[52] "Philosophie première, philosophie seconde et métaphysique chez Aristote." In: *Revue philosophique de Louvain*, 56, 1958, p. 165-221.

[53] W. D. Ross: *Aristotle's Metaphysics.* Oxford, 1924, Vol. I, p. 253 is also of the

Reflecting on the problem from the standpoint of history of ideas, P. Aubenque [54] likewise comes to the conclusion that Aristotelian metaphysics is neither simply an ontology nor simply a theology. According to Aubenque, it is a "science without a name" which necessarily wavers between being defined as ontology on the one hand, and theology, on the other, without ever being able to be unified. As "First Philosophy" or "theology" it claims to be the science of the *arche*, the determining origin or cause of beings. It cannot grasp this origin and cause on its own, however, but only by means of something which has already been "originated" and caused. Nevertheless, any attempt which seeks to grasp the cause of being at its origin, through the mediation of something movable, must founder. Knowledge of the origin must itself be "original" knowledge; the being of the cause itself as something *un-mediated* can only be given in the immediate contemplation of this cause itself. But any attempt to ground being in a universal science of Being must founder as well. The science of being as being seeks to establish the unity of being from the diversity of the ways of speaking of Being. But the "science in question" can only "signify" the One and the unity assured by it through the mediation of language and it remains in the only realm of being accessible to man, that of sublunar (movable, sensible) beings. As such it proves incapable of including the divine being, separate from that realm, in the universal it seeks. Thus Aubenque comes to the conclusion that Aristotelian metaphysics remains aporetic. In sustaining this aporia, it forms its own "method" of tentative inquiry — the "method" of dialectics.

Considering the status of scholarship sketched above, one is forced to the position that an unambiguous solution to the questions concerning the relationship of Books Epsilon and Kappa to Book Gamma is impossible. H. Wagner [55] recognized this clearly; he maintained that although

opinion that "both views are generally Aristotelian" yet holds that the theological view is more strongly supported in Aristotle's works as a whole.

According to S. Moser: *Metaphysik einst und jetzt.* Berlin, 1958, the science of being as being is — similarly to the understanding of the Scholastics — on the one hand a science of the universal in being as the highest conceivable universal, and on the other hand a theology, and as such the science of a particular concrete being. In this very "contradiction" Moser sees the fitting expression of Aristotle's aporetic philosophizing. At the same time, he supports the thesis that theology has "precedence" over ontology.

[54] *La théorie de l'être chez Aristote.* Paris, 1962.

[55] Cf. Part Three, n. 39.

much has been clarified by contemporary scholarship, even with regard to Book Gamma, in relation to other questions "all clear footholds vanish" (p. 145). In particular, he comments: "A compelling proof that the *prote ousia* (the express concern in 1005 a 35) can also be conceived in Gamma as it is defined without a doubt, in Epsilon 1 is impossible. Unfortunately!"

In concluding let us remember that for our part we have answered in a particular sense the question of the character of Aristotle's philosophical theory. In this investigation we began with Book Gamma. In the preface we mentioned two reasons for this. One was that in Book Gamma Aristotle defined the "program" of metaphysics; the other was that only in this book is the "one, certain nature" defined, whose principles and highest causes are in question. Then, following this program, we pursued the definitions of *ousia*, in Books Zeta, Eta, and Theta. In the course of this, it appeared to us that in its meaning, the Aristotelian ontology is an ousiology. At the same time, however, in expounding the concepts of this ousiology, we were led — as if it were inevitable — to theology. For in the key concepts of ousiology, in *energeia* and *dynamis*, emerges a priority of the *energeia*. This priority of *energeia* then culminates in the determination of God as a first being, as an entity prior as such, for Aristotle conceives of God as *energeia* freed from all *dynamis*.

From this we concluded that theology is the ultimate fulfilment of ousiology. In this sense, we spoke of theology as being the "keystone" of philosophical theory in the sense of ousiology (see above, p. 13). The train of thought implies that basic concepts developed in Aristotle's ousiology require a theology. This is not meant to bear upon the history of the development of Aristotle's philosophy — Book Lambda was written before Gamma, Zeta, Eta, and Theta.[56] But this means that the priority of *energeia* to *dynamis* needs to be justified. Such a justification can be found in the fact that Aristotle thought of a "best" being to be defined as pure *energeia*. Without this justification — as furnished by theology — the priority of *energeia* to *dynamis* in ousiology would have remained a mere assertion.

With regard to this position, one could perhaps object that it makes Aristotle a "builder of systems." We share the prevailing view, however, that Aristotle's philosophy is not "systematic" in the modern sense, but aporetic. Seeing this, however, does not prohibit us from pointing out a connection when one emerges from a train of thought by necessity,

---

[56] Düring, *op. cit.*, p. 593.

particularly when it then opens a horizon for exegetical investigations. When the fundamental concepts of ousiology are thought through to the end, a connection becomes apparent between Aristotle's ontology and theology. Thus, on these grounds one can assert with great probability that God, as the cause of everything else also is one of the "principles and causes" of the "one, certain nature" which must be investigated by the theoretician, according to the "program" outlined in Book Gamma. Taken in this way, the theoretician who, according to Book Gamma, seeks the causes and principles of *ousia*, as an ousiologist, is also a theologian.

Perhaps one can go one step further: one must consider what it really means for the total conception of Aristotle's metaphysics that he conceived of the pure actuality and perfection of the highest being *not* as the "actualization" of a potential,[57] but as independence from the order of becoming and of time, as a principle and — to use a modern expression — as an "absolute." To be sure, Aristotle did not conceive of the actual Being of God "Platonically" as a kind of "idea," but as an activeness forming transient beings and individuals.[58] Does not the fact that Aristotle's thinking took the absolute, actual and active Being of God as its starting-point imply a distinctive significance of his theology for ontology? Would Aristotle have been able to address his inquiry to those characteristics of transient beings which are removed from all change and all passing away (*hyle* and *eidos*, *ti en einai* and *energeia*, substance and categories) if he had not found in the concept of *energeia*, conceived of as a principle and as an "absolute," the concept in which he conceives of the quality of the divine, if he had not found there some kind of "cause" or "ground" bearing those abiding aspects? One can pose this question even when one admits that Aristotle himself nowhere explicitly draws the connection between the concepts which form the framework for his thinking about God in his theology and the objects of his thinking in ousiology. Might one be able to refer again to the passage cited above from Theta 8:[59] "If

---

[57] In a "cosmological" deliberation Aristotle excluded the possibility that Being in its entirety originates from a potentiality, as this was assumed in various Greek theogonies and cosmogonies. For cosmology, everything had arisen out of the "chaos and the night" (1071 b 26 ff. and 1072 a 19 f.). Aristotle, however, rejected, especially on ontological grounds, this doctrine of the physicians, according to whom "all things were there together potentially" (1069 b 23) and did this by conceiving of God as principally, absolutely existent.

[58] Cf. on this point 1071 b 14 ff.

[59] 1050 b 19.

these [read: the divinities] did not exist, nothing at all would exist"? And may we take it principally as an indication that for Aristotle God is the *arche* also in the sense of a "presupposition" — in modern terms: a "condition for the possibility" — for every *ousia*? In any case, in this thought of the "absolute" actual Being of God, in this primacy of the divine as a principle, we see the peculiarity which characterizes the connection between the two doctrines of *ousia*, on the one hand, and of the divine, on the other. The consequence inherent in Aristotle's thought appears to us to lie in the fact that by virtue of this connection, ousiology took on a theological "meaning," and it was this inherent consequence which then found its realization in the history of our metaphysical tradition.

INDEX